A NEW BIRTH
OF FREEDOM

A NEW BIRTH OF FREEDOM

LINCOLN AT GETTYSBURG

BY

PHILIP B. KUNHARDT, JR.

Little, Brown and Company   Boston   Toronto

FIRST EDITION

Unless otherwise credited, all illustrations in this book appear courtesy of The Dorothy Meserve Kunhardt Trust. Many of the pictures were printed from original Mathew Brady negatives in the Meserve Collection, which formerly belonged to Mrs. Kunhardt and now reside at the National Portrait Gallery in Washington, D.C.

Library of Congress Cataloging in Publication Data

Kunhardt, Philip B.
  A new birth of freedom.

  Includes index.
  1. Lincoln, Abraham, 1809–1865 — Journeys — Pennsylvania — Gettysburg. 2. Gettysburg, Battle of, 1863.
I. Title.
E475.55.L76K86 1983   973.7'349   83-16167
ISBN 0-316-50600-1

MU

Designed by Susan Windheim
Production coordinated by Dede Cummings

*Published simultaneously in Canada
by Little, Brown & Company (Canada) Limited*

PRINTED IN THE UNITED STATES OF AMERICA

PREFACE

My grandfather was born the year Lincoln was killed. As a young man he set out to illustrate his father's Civil War diary and soon became a collector and preserver of nineteenth-century American photographs, with a special, almost fanatic interest in the more than one hundred photographic images of Abraham Lincoln that were scattered here and there, many on their way to being lost or forgotten had he not sought them out. Frederick Hill Meserve died at the age of ninety-six twenty-two years ago, leaving the famous Meserve Collection to his three children, two of whom generously gave their shares to the third, a Lincoln zealot like her father — my mother.

She had a very special feeling for Mr. Lincoln (she always called him that) — very formal their relationship, but he was someone she felt she knew well, a person of flesh and blood and laughter for whom she cared very much. To her the self-educated prairie lawyer who became President and freed the slaves was a lot more than a fascinating historical figure, and he certainly wasn't the perfect, all-wise, Godlike figure that time and too much reverence had made of him. Instead, she could practically hear his high-pitched, raspy voice, practically share his gloom one minute and catch the mirthful glint of his blue-gray eyes the next. Her insatiable curiosity about her friend was at least part of the reason she bypassed her extremely successful career as an author of children's books to concentrate on making herself an imaginative and unique Lincoln scholar. Dorothy Kunhardt, the writer of such classics as *Junket Is Nice* and *Pat the Bunny*, reinstated her maiden name and became Dorothy Meserve Kunhardt, the historian.

So even though it was New Jersey, I grew up in Lincoln land. My mother would set out for secondhand bookstores almost every day and come back laden with new source material on Lincoln, which she would devour all night long. A new packet of pictures would always be arriving in our mailbox, marked "Meserve Collection" in the corner, with a note signed "Pa" inside; my grandfather had made a new discovery, had identified a face, had found a clue to the story a picture told, lurking in the shadows of the emulsion of one of his Mathew Brady negatives. Growing up in this atmosphere, how could I have failed to succumb? Soon I was reading the books too, and starting collections of my own.

My mother and I collaborated on a number of Lincoln projects. In the early 1960s we traveled to Springfield, Illinois, to do research on Lincoln's hometown and the tomb in which he is buried. Together we wrote *Twenty Days* (published in 1965), a book about Lincoln's assassination and the time just following. In the middle of this project, my mother took time out to write a magazine article on the Gettysburg Address, to appear on the speech's hundredth anniversary. Afterward she was asked to expand the article into a short book. That excited her; she would do it as soon as she had the time. But the time never seemed to come and the years began to creep up on her.

In 1976, three years before she died, we collaborated once more — on *Mathew Brady and His World*, a book that included many of the rare photographs from the Meserve Collection. Soon after, my mother asked me if writing a Gettysburg book interested me. It did. But I had in mind a somewhat different book than she did; there were things that I, personally, wanted to tell about Lincoln. The President's journey to Pennsylvania and the speech he gave there seemed to offer a perfect narrative framework not only for exploring Lincoln's mind but for examining certain aspects of his life that seemed especially important then and still do today.

From the beginning it has been my hope to excite readers across the land as they get acquainted with a thin but fascinating slice of their country's remarkable past. *A New Birth of Freedom* springs out of literally hundreds upon hundreds of source books, as well as newspapers, magazines, and other journals of the day, letters, diaries, memoirs, scrapbooks, privately held records, and hitherto unused notes of several authoritative scholars (in particular, my mother). Even though no footnotes appear on these pages, what follows is the most thoroughly researched and accurate account of Lincoln's trip to Gettysburg, the days preceding the trip, and the writing of the famous speech, that I could make 120 years after the events took place.

A NEW BIRTH
OF FREEDOM

ONE

ACTUALLY, if Mary Lincoln had got her way, her husband would never have made the trip to Gettysburg at all. The first couple of the land had awakened on this Wednesday morning in November with not only their ten-year-old son Tad sick and miserable but the President himself feeling bilious and out of sorts. Only yesterday Tad had been his usual irrepressible self, charging down the main hallway of the White House living quarters, making a racetrack out of the corridor for his wagons, and for horse contests, too, whenever he could persuade his father to take him up on his back and become a galloping steed.

Now Mrs. Lincoln was insistent that there be no trip to Gettysburg. Only yesterday she had canceled her plans to go; her husband must now do likewise. It was unthinkable that a father would leave a child who was in danger. When Mrs. Lincoln demanded something that

Mary Lincoln tried her hardest to keep the President from going to Gettysburg. Here she is shown still dressed in mourning for her son Willie over a year after his death. But even in her tormented state she could not refrain from wearing her beloved jewelry, which dripped from her ears, neck, waist, wrists, and fingers for Mathew Brady's camera.

she knew would be as difficult to win as this, she did it hysterically; and hysterics with her meant acting out a true child's tantrum — even to the point of rolling on the floor and pulling her hair — until her disturbed husband gave in. She showed no shame at her lack of self-discipline, just an insane desperation to get her husband to stay and tend to Tad. She was a poor nurse herself — one instant filled with a terror that communicated itself to the patient, the next moment laughing and gossiping with a visitor, the child forgotten.

But today President Lincoln was determined that his agitated wife would not get her way. He knew how important the Gettysburg dedication was: not only important to the many people who had worked long and hard arranging the day's events and to the parents and wives and children of the many men who had died in the battle, but important to the nation, too — important to the spirit with which the war must be pursued. Lincoln had something special he wanted to say in Pennsylvania, something that had been a long time brewing, something that, he hoped, would make a difference.

⋘══════⋙

Eighteen sixty-three was the year — not long ago as the history of countries is measured. Henry Ford was born that year, and so was newspaper baron William Randolph Hearst. Sam Houston died in 1863. It was the year margarine was invented, by a French chemist; the year the world's first subway was introduced, in London; and it was the year an iron scoop was fitted to a steam engine to create the cowcatcher — in America, naturally. Also in America, 1863 was the year wheels were attached to shoes, and lo and behold — roller skates!

Overseas, it was the era of Dickens, Thackeray, Ibsen, Dostoevski, Tolstoy; of Ingres and Daumier; of Berlioz and Brahms. And, at home, a new and vital kind of writing was emerging, led by Whitman, Dickinson, Melville, Emerson, Twain, and Thoreau. Winslow Homer and

James Whistler were still in their twenties; and Stephen Foster, approaching the end of his life, had composed the first truly American music. It couldn't be recorded yet — Thomas Edison was only a tinkering teenager.

Eighteen sixty-three was the third year Abraham Lincoln had been President of the United States. And it was also the third year of America's Civil War. During the first days of July a mighty battle had been fought between massive armies of the North and the South in and around a small Pennsylvania town called Gettysburg. It was to become the decisive battle of the war, guaranteeing ultimate victory for the young, expanding country that claimed freedom and equality were for all its inhabitants, and insuring ultimate defeat for the states that had decided to withhold those rights from certain individuals.

Four and a half months after that great battle, a pleasant November week got underway in the nation's capital. Some citizens might have been surprised to read the latest claim of the great English scientist Sir John Herschel. The sun was a planet, he announced, populated by inhabitants who were able to survive because they were insensitive to their planet's rays. It was a week when the city of Saint Louis was finding it had a nasty smallpox epidemic on its hands, while in Boston citizens were rejoicing over a grand new organ that had arrived for their Music Hall. *Lucrezia Borgia* was the opera packing them in at Wallach's Theater in New York City. On a more personal plane, at the African Church in Petersburg, Virginia, Major J. J. Vorhines, the celebrated Kentucky dwarf, was marrying his sweetheart — two-foot-two-inch Ella Sawyer.

On Wednesday, the eighteenth day of this November, General Ulysses S. Grant was in Chattanooga, Tennessee, preparing Union attacks on the Confederate strongholds at Lookout Mountain and Missionary Ridge, the two heights commanding that city. Chattanooga had suddenly become central in the war. Great armies had been advancing, building bridges along the way, transporting supplies and ammunition over the mountain ranges, across the rivers and streams. Two hundred thousand soldiers were coming together from east and west to fight the battle, to take the high ground away from the Confederates. On this Wednesday, General Grant telegraphed back to Washington: "Sherman's advance reached Lookout Mountain today. Movements will progress. . . ." That day the written orders were issued to Generals William Tecumseh Sherman and George Henry Thomas for the battle that lay just ahead.

On this particular Wednesday in November the nation was eighty-seven years old. It could still remember firsthand from a few and second-hand from many the revolution that had brought it into being, could still feel some of its birth pangs, could remember the faces and handshakes of its founding fathers. The West was still practically untouched, stretching endlessly it seemed, waiting to be opened and tamed. There were mountains to conquer, great rivers to harness, rails to lay, vast stretches of land to plant, gold and silver and coal and black showers of oil to discover. Americans were absorbed with themselves and their bounteous land. It was a matter of very little concern to any of them that, as the newspapers reported, the world just then could count 1.288 billion inhabitants who spoke over three thousand different languages. People were not surprised that the average age at death for a U.S. citizen was only twenty-seven; that's the way it was — God had made it so.

It was on this particular November Wednesday, too, that President Lincoln was scheduled to leave by train for Gettysburg. Plans called for him to stay there overnight. The following day — Thursday, the nineteenth — he would participate in the dedication of a national cemetery where Union soldiers who had died at Gettysburg were being buried.

After the great battle the previous summer, the little town of Gettysburg had turned into a huge, insane emergency field-hospital. Almost every

LEFT & OPPOSITE: *Working for Alexander Gardner at the time, Timothy O'Sullivan was traveling with the Army of the Potomac when the shooting started at Gettysburg. Gardner joined him before the battle was over, and their views were among the most poignant of the entire war. They made vivid forever the commonplace sites where so many brave men had fallen. These three scenes were taken in the Wheat-Field (top left), in front of Little Round Top (bottom left), and at the Slaughter-Pen.*

structure that could give shelter had been filled to overflowing with the wounded — private houses, barns, sheds, churches, taverns, hotels, even the general stores, the schoolhouse, the seminary, the college, the court-house. Northerners and Southerners lay side by side, treated, if they were lucky, by one of the 106 medical officers General George Gordon Meade had left behind; of these, only one-third were surgeons. Volunteers acted as nurses, joining the military musicians who manned the ambulances along with paroled Confederate prisoners. Long tables, set up in the woods, were used for operating. "For seven days it literally ran blood," wrote a nurse who attended the surgery. Wagons were loaded to over-flowing with amputated arms and legs, then driven off, emptied into trenches, and returned for more.

RIGHT: *Scenes like this stereoscopic "candid" were easy to come by for photographers roaming the Gettysburg battlefields after the fighting. In more than half the cases, legs hit by musket balls during the Civil War were treated by amputation.*

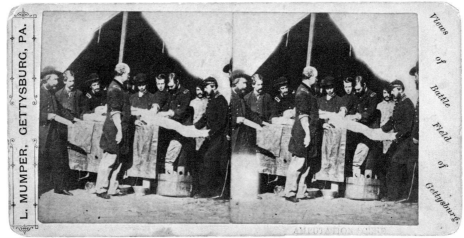

The numbers were staggering. For the Union army, 23,000 either killed or wounded; for the Confederates, 28,000. Some 20,000 injured were still alive, and their cries of pain and anguish made a wailing, screeching chorus over the land. Preachers read the Twenty-third Psalm over and over again as fast as their lips could say it, while soldier after soldier expired. The dead lay everywhere — in the fields, on the hillsides, beneath the trees of the shattered woods. Families of soldiers lost in action searched pathetically amid the bodies.

Adding to this pool of agony, this ocean of unbearable sights, portions of half-buried corpses could be seen poking from the earth. On the Fourth of July, hours before the Confederates had finally retreated, a fierce rain had almost drowned many of the wounded who lay on low ground; it had also washed away most of the topsoil from the shallow graves in which the first days' fallen had been speedily buried during lulls in the fighting, leaving exposed arms or legs or even bloated heads. The swollen bodies of thousands of dead horses added to the cursed scene. After the rains, the July temperature rose. The days blazed. Ripples of heat undulated off the fields. Soon the entire town and the fighting areas

OPPOSITE: *Killed on the first day of fighting at Gettysburg, Confederate dead lay in their shallow common grave with boards at their heads to mark their identities.*

A young Gettysburg attorney and one of its leading citizens, David Wills was appointed to see that the dead were buried in all haste and the town cleansed.

for miles around reeked unbearably. One nurse wrote home that the sickening stench could be "cut with a knife." Approaching the normally bucolic village was like entering a slaughterhouse. To prevent gagging, people held smelling salts or sticks of camphor to their noses. Pestilence and vermin were feared.

In was upon this wretched scene that Andrew Curtin, governor of Pennsylvania, gazed when he arrived to see what could be done for the disaster area. Appalled, Curtin soon appointed a young Gettysburg lawyer named David Wills to be in charge locally. Wills was a logical choice; he was able, energetic, wealthy, and public-spirited. Curtin empowered Wills to do anything to cleanse the town and bury the dead as quickly as possible.

At first, field burial seemed too impermanent; Wills decided early that his small labor force would try to box the corpses individually. Those with identification would be shipped to their families. But after seven hundred bodies had been boxed, the volunteers gave up; the heat and the smell were just too much. Instead, they resumed digging graves next to where the bodies lay.

Sometime during this grim aftermath of battle, a national cemetery, right on the fighting ground, was suggested. A sacred resting place. A suitable memorial. As for the Confederate dead, trenches could be dug and a hundred or more buried at once. But for the dead from the eighteen Union states that had participated in the battle, something grand and permanent should be created. It sounded just right.

When Wills had made the appropriate overtures and received approval for the idea, he picked out some land adjacent to the town's regular cemetery and work began. Back in Washington, Lincoln was told about these plans and approved.

Aloof and lacking glitter, Robert Todd was Lincoln's first-born — but certainly not his favorite. Here he posed while a boarding student at Phillips Exeter Academy in New Hampshire. (The case has been removed in this copy of the ambrotype.)

TWO

IT was not an easy decision for Lincoln to leave Tad behind in his sickbed and go off to Gettysburg. The Lincolns had had four children — all boys — and two of them had died of lung infections (probably pneumonia) that could not be treated properly.

Robert was their first child, a baby who cried a great deal at the Globe Tavern in Springfield where his parents went to live after their wedding. Not much is known of Robert in his first years, or of Edward, who followed him. When Eddie (or Eddy, as the Lincolns sometimes spelled it) was born, Lincoln wrote to his friend Joshua Speed:

We have another boy, born the 10th of March last. He is very much such a child as Bob was at his age — rather of a *longer* order. Bob is 'short and low,' and, I expect, always will be. He talks very plainly — almost as plainly as any body. He is quite smart enough. I some times fear he is one of the little rare-ripe sort, that are smarter at about five than ever after. He has a great deal of that sort of mischief, that is the offspring of much animal spirits. Since I began this letter a messenger came to tell me, Bob was lost; but by the time I reached the house, his mother had found him, and had him whip[p]ed — and, by now, very likely he is run away again.

The attitude of both Abraham and Mary Lincoln toward their children was one of extreme indulgence; they adored their sons and scarcely ever corrected them, feeling that they would grow out of any little tricks or troublesomeness and that the most important thing was to be sure that their childhood was uncloudedly happy.

When Lincoln was serving as a U.S. congressman in 1848, he discussed family matters in a letter to his wife, who was dividing her time between her family in Lexington, Kentucky, and her husband in Washington.

Dear Eddy thinks father is "gone tapila" [probably baby talk for "gone to the capital"]. I went yesterday to hunt the little plaid stockings, as you wished; but found that McKnight has quit business, and Allen had not a single pair of the description you give, and only one plaid pair of any sort that I thought would fit "Eddy's dear little feet." I have a notion to make another trial tomorrow morning. . . . I did not get rid of the impression of that foolish dream about dear Bobby till I got your letter written the same day. What did he and Eddy think of the little letters father sent them? Don't let the blessed fellows forget father.

Another letter, addressed to "My Dear Wife," concluded: "By the way, you do not intend to do without a girl, because the one you had has left you? Get another as soon as you can to take charge of the dear codgers. Father expected to see you all sooner; but let it pass; stay as long as you please. . . . Kiss and love the dear rascals."

But one of the dear rascals was not to live. With Lincoln's congressional term completed, the family was together in Springfield in late 1849; but on February 1, 1850, only a few weeks before his fourth birthday, Eddie, who adored kittens and whose face lit up when he heard the word *Father*, finally succumbed after fighting fever and consumption for fifty-two days. On the night before the child's demise, Lincoln dreamed his strange, recurrent dream of impending death: he saw himself sailing swiftly on an unknown ship, toward an unknown shore.

Lincoln wrote that "we lost our little boy . . . not our first, but our second child. We miss him very much." The loss was indeed a terrible blow to both parents, and ten years after Eddie's death, Mary Lincoln still burst into wild tears at the mention of his name.

So when Willie was born just ten months after the family tragedy, it was almost as if Eddie had been reborn. At least he made the Lincolns forget. Quiet, bright, thoughtful, and possessed of a wonderful memory, Willie was Lincoln's favorite. He and Tad — Thomas, the Lincolns' fourth and last child, who they had hoped so much would be a girl — were the delight of their father; they could do no wrong. With Robert away at school in the East, these two scamps practically ran the white frame house in Springfield on the corner of Eighth and Jackson streets. They were in and out of their father's law office even when he was interviewing important clients. They raised cain the town over — and Lincoln would only smile. When the family moved to Washington and the White House, nothing changed. The two little boys had a heyday exploring the old mansion, giving plays in its attic, making friends with the soldiers who guarded their father, even breaking into cabinet meetings.

And then it all happened again. Eleven-year-old Willie caught cold riding his pony on the White House grounds in the winter slosh, and on February 20, 1862, he died. This time the Lincolns' grief was uncontrollable. When Eddie had expired more than a decade before, Mary Lincoln had refused to eat but her husband had tried to console her, saying, "Mary, we must live!" Now his grief was beyond control and

Studious and charming, William Wallace was Lincoln's third son, born ten months after the death of the second — three-year-old Eddie. Willie died in the White House, apparently of pneumonia, early in 1862. Here he is shown posed at Brady's Gallery.

Mary abandoned herself completely to anguish. For her it was the beginning of a long, downward slide that would end in insanity. Already there were intimations. During a particularly wild outburst, Lincoln led his wife to the window and pointed to the lunatic asylum. "Mother, do you see that large white building on the hill yonder?" he said. "Try and control your grief, or it will drive you mad, and we may have to send you there."

At first Lincoln himself could not speak at all. His whole body was racked and shaken by sobs. His mourning went on and on, even after the funeral was long over. Months later, reading Shakespeare with a friend, he broke down over a passage in which a mother mourns for her son. "Did you ever dream of some lost friend," Lincoln asked in a voice that trembled, "and feel that you were having a sweet communion with him, and yet have a consciousness that it is not a reality? That is the way I dream of my lost boy Willie." Then Lincoln sat with his head bowed down on the table and wept convulsively.

Mary Lincoln, who was too distraught to attend Willie's funeral, remained in seclusion in the White House for an unexpectedly long period. In her opinion the Lord had sent this punishment to warn her that she was paying too much attention to worldly matters. And perhaps she and her husband had idolized the boys too much. She had just enough strength to sit up in bed and paste accounts of the tragedy into a scrapbook. She read over many times the words of the writer Nathaniel P. Willis, who had pleased her so when he said he found her conversation fascinating.

"This little fellow had his acquaintances among his father's friends, and I chanced to be one of them," Willis wrote of Willie.

He never failed to seek me out in the crowd and shake hands and make some pleasant remark. But he had more than mere affectionateness. His self-possession — aplomb as the French call it — was extraordinary. I was one day passing the White House, when he was outside with a playfellow on the

Nathaniel P. Willis, who wrote so glowingly of Willie

sidewalk. [Secretary of State William] Seward drove in with Prince Napoleon and two of his suite in the carriage; and, in a mock heroic way — terms of amusing intimacy evidently existing between the boy and the Secretary — the official gentleman took off his hat, and Napoleon did the same, all making the young prince President a ceremonious salute. Not a bit staggered with the homage, Willie drew himself up to his full height, took off his little cap with graceful self-possession, and bowed down formally to the ground, like a little ambassador. They drove past, and he went on unconcernedly with his play. . . . His genial and open expression of countenance was none the less ingenuous and fearless for a certain tincture of fun; and it was in this mingling of qualities that he so faithfully resembled his father.

With all the splendor that was around this little fellow in his new home, he was so bravely and beautifully himself — and that only! A wildflower transplanted from the prairie to a hot house, he retained his prairie habits, unalterably *pure* and simple, till he died.

More welcome to Mary Lincoln even than glowing words were the visits of a new friend, a practicing spiritualist. She listened carefully to the messages she received from Willie by means of tappings and scrapings on furniture in her bedroom. She heard whole sentences when the medium went into a trance — messages that were not completely satisfactory, since they were not coming to her in Willie's own voice but in the strange tones of the medium's "control."

Mary had visions of Willie as well as audible messages. She told her visiting half sister that "he comes to me every night, and stands at the foot of my bed with the same sweet adorable smile. . . . Little Eddie is sometimes with him."

With Willie and Eddie dead and Robert, whom Lincoln could never really warm to, away now at Harvard, the President became more and more attached to his "Tadpole," the last-born — and the most difficult. Even when Willie was alive, the bond between Tad and his father had been close. Back in Springfield people could remember Lincoln sitting in a rocker and, in his tone-deaf voice, tenderly singing a hymn to quiet his youngest son.

Jesus, my all, to heav'n is gone,
He whom I fix my hopes upon;
His track I see, and I'll pursue
The narrow way till him I view.

Unlike Willie, Tad was neither brilliant nor good-looking. His speech was almost incomprehensible because of a cleft in the roof of his mouth. He sounded adenoidal. Even when his photograph was taken and he was posed to look his best, his mouth remained open just a crack. Mischievous and unruly, with a head too large for his body and a mind that never stopped thinking up new and naughtier things to do, Tad romped through the White House as if it were a gigantic playhouse

Mischievous and spoiled, Thomas — Tad, for short — was the youngest Lincoln, the fourth boy. A frequent visitor at the Brady gallery in Washington, Tad was here photographed squirmed up in the chair in which his father often posed. Tad's illness made Lincoln think twice about going to Gettysburg.

constructed just for him. He dragged wagons through its corridors, bounced on the state furniture, locked important doors when they needed to be opened, yanked at bell cords, ordered servants about, used the guards as his personal emissaries, hooked goldfish in the greenhouse tank with bent pins, remodeled the ornate chairs with his penknife, made the firehoses into weapons, and set up a store in the White House lobby, making cabinet members and congressmen buy his wares as they entered to see his father. Lincoln just smiled and took Tad everywhere with him — on interviews, visits, trips, even to the battlefields. When Tad ignored his tutor, Lincoln said: "Let him run. There's time enough yet for him to learn his letters and get pokey." Punishment was unthinkable. Even a cabinet meeting came to a halt when Tad broke in to request of his father some slight favor. Never tell Lincoln a secret, people said;

The White House grounds were perfect for playing — plenty of running room and trees to climb. Tad is thought to be the child perched on the wall in the right foreground of this picture.

he can't keep it — he'll tell Tad. At night Tad would fall asleep beneath the President's chair, and when Lincoln was finally done with affairs of state, he would carry his son to bed. It was not only Tad whom Lincoln was adoring; it was Eddie and Willie as well.

How to reach beyond all the ghastliness left by the battle at Gettysburg and find words that would give hope for the future! Lincoln had gone down on his knees in his room during those first days of July and asked God not to let the nation perish. He had tried his best, but the burden was more than he could bear. Miraculously, as he was still imploring God to help the country, he felt that all of a sudden he was being answered. And from then on he had had no doubt as to the outcome of the battle. This had been Lincoln's private, almost unbelievable adventure of the spirit. Now, almost five months later, divine help could — would — come again and direct him how to communicate to the people assembling at Gettysburg. Already he had the gist of what he might say — the ideas, a lot of the words he would use. God would help him with the rest.

This morning, with the Gettysburg trip only hours away, Lincoln was unable to persuade Tad to take a bite of breakfast. The boy had always eaten for him; he was surely sick. Medicines were on the way from Thompson's drugstore across the street from the Treasury Building, and the doctor was expected. Even so, Lincoln knew he must go to Pennsylvania.

THREE

EVER since those three days of unprecedented fighting at Gettysburg, Lincoln had wanted to address the country. He had made a solemn promise to himself to make a special public summing-up of what he passionately felt about the nation, what it meant to die for it, and the obligations those deaths left behind for the living. His first public words on this subject were spoken four days after the Gettysburg victory, on the evening of July 7. The invasion of the North by General Robert E. Lee's army had been repulsed, and news of another great victory — this one at Vicksburg, on the Mississippi — had just arrived that day. A crowd in a festive mood had gathered outside the White House to serenade the President. Lincoln was called upon to speak.

"I do most sincerely thank Almighty God," his shrill, high voice pierced the warm night air, "for the occasion on which you have called. How long ago is it?

— eighty-odd years — since on the Fourth of July for the first time in the history of the world a nation by its representatives, assembled and declared as a self-evident truth that 'all men are created equal.' " For a moment Lincoln paused. Then, after speaking of Jefferson and Adams and, finally, the recent victory at Gettysburg, he quickly closed: "Gentlemen, this is a glorious theme, and the occasion for a speech, but I am not prepared to make one worthy of the occasion. . . . Having said this much, I will now take the music."

With Lee's defeated army on the run — virtually trapped in Northern territory by the temporarily uncrossable Potomac, swollen by the heavy rains — the war could actually be brought to its conclusion now by one last mighty Union attack. If General Meade gathered his victorious Army of the Potomac at Gettysburg and followed the tattered and suffering Confederates south to the river, it would all be over. Lincoln at first assumed that was what was going to happen.

"It is certain," he wrote on July 11, "that after three days fighting at Gettysburg, Lee withdrew and made for the Potomac; that he found the river so swollen as to prevent his crossing; that he is still this side near Hagerstown and Williamsport, preparing to defend himself; and that Meade is close upon him preparing to attack him."

The following day Meade had not yet struck and Lincoln paced the floor of the telegraph office in the War Department, agitated by Meade's latest dispatch stating his "intention to attack the enemy tomorrow, unless something intervenes." Lincoln wrung his hands, murmuring "too late" and "they will be ready to fight a magnificent battle when there is no enemy to fight."

Two days later, just before a scheduled cabinet meeting, Lincoln received the news that Lee had indeed crossed the Potomac and escaped into Virginia, and that Meade's attack had never come. At 1:00 P.M. that day, a telegram went out to Meade under the name of Lincoln's main military adviser, General-in-Chief Henry Halleck. "The enemy should be pursued and cut up, wherever he may have gone. . . . I need hardly say to you that the escape of Lee's army without another battle has created great dissatisfaction in the mind of the President, and it will require an active and energetic pursuit on your part to remove the impression that it has not been sufficiently active heretofore."

It took Meade only an hour and a half to reply to "Old Brains," that tentative, petulant, and highly disliked commander who was always all for winning just so long as there was no risk involved. (Lincoln once

General George Gordon Meade had been handed the command of the Army of the Potomac only three days before the firing at Gettysburg began.

said that he had befriended Halleck because the general had no other friends.) Actually, Meade knew whom he was really answering, although he could not know that at that very moment the Commander in Chief lay prone on a sofa at the War Department, deeply depressed and annoyed beyond words.

"The censure of the President," said Meade, ". . . is, in my judgment, so undeserved that I feel compelled most respectfully to ask to be immediately relieved from the command of this army."

Lincoln would not accept the resignation, but Meade's enraged request did cause the President to write the general a harsh letter of explanation.

"I do not believe," the letter said in part, "you appreciate the magnitude of the misfortune involved in Lee's escape. He was within your easy grasp, and to have closed upon him would, in connection with our other late successes, have ended the war. As it is, the war will be prolonged indefinitely. . . . Your golden opportunity is gone, and I am distressed immeasurably because of it."

Although he had second thoughts and never sent the letter, on the following day Lincoln was still angry. "If I had gone up there," he said to his son Robert, "I could have whipped them myself."

<hr />

When would the proper time arrive to put into words for his fellow countrymen what he was feeling in his soul? Even though his spirits had begun to rise again, the long, hot summer would not present a suitable occasion. Mrs. Lincoln and Tad escaped the August heat of the capital — and the ever-feared sickness that could be the result — by making a trip north to New Hampshire and the White Mountains, and then to Vermont, before returning to Washington in late September. Lincoln's telegrams and letters to his wandering wife were businesslike, warming when they referred to Tad. "All as well as usual," the President wrote on August 8, "and no particular trouble any way. . . . Tell dear Tad, poor 'Nanny Goat' is lost; and Mrs. Cuthbert [Mary Ann Cuthbert, seamstress, then "stewardess" of the White House] & I are in distress about it. The day you left Nanny was found resting herself, and chewing her little cud, on the middle of Tad's bed. But now she's gone. . . . The weather continues dry, and excessively warm here. . . . But enough. Affectionately."

To escape the city's heat, after the day was finished Lincoln usually rode out to a large cottage reserved for the President on the grounds of

Latticed railings and trellises adorned the front porch of the President's summer retreat, a cottage beside the Soldiers' Home just north of the capital. While Lincoln was riding unattended to this house one evening, a sniper shot a bullet through his hat.

the Soldiers' Home. In the past he had sometimes made the three-mile trip to the northern outskirts of the city unguarded, taking a carriage or riding horseback. But this summer Secretary of War Edwin Stanton was insisting that the President be accompanied. So was Lincoln's "particular friend" Ward Hill Lamon, who had been railing against these solo rides and the chief executive's general lack of protection. To Lamon, Lincoln playfully replied that the only way to keep the President safe was to lock him up in an iron box — but then how would he fulfill his duties? "If they kill me, the next man will be just as bad for them," Lincoln joshed.

Stanton and Lamon prevailed, however. Often on August mornings early risers in Washington were treated to the clatter of approaching hooves and the sight of a tall figure dressed in black riding by on a gray horse. They would know immediately who it was by the lieutenant with yellow stripes riding beside him; then, two by two, there followed two dozen or more cavalry, sabers drawn and held upright.

The war consumed most of Lincoln's waking hours. The little pins on the maps in his office kept changing place as armies on the move took up new positions. Telegrams arrived from commanders in the field, and Lincoln often answered them himself, in crisp, direct, and graphic terms. Whereas at the beginning of the war it was sometimes difficult at cabinet meetings to tell who was in command, now Lincoln ruled with absolute authority, looking to each cabinet member for his special brand of wisdom but retaining the decision-making power for himself alone.

August brought a few diversions. Lincoln learned how to assemble the new Spencer automatic rifle and then had some target practice with it. He posed for several photographs at the studio of James and Alexander Gardner. He listened, along with the cabinet, to General Meade describing what the fighting had been like at Gettysburg. He visited the old naval observatory at Twenty-seventh and E streets, NW. He read Shakespeare to his young personal secretary John Hay far into the night

OPPOSITE: *Taken shortly after the end of the battle, this peaceful view of Gettysburg showed none of the panic its citizens were feeling.*

at the Soldiers' Home. But these were the exceptions; work was the rule. Of all his chores, the business of pardons was the most burdensome and draining. Diligently Lincoln studied case histories, often calling for additional information before passing judgment on men's lives.

A different kind of summer was unfolding a bit north and west in the town of Gettysburg.

"Men, horses and wagons wanted immediately to bury the dead and to cleanse our streets," pleaded a notice in Gettysburg's *Adams Sentinel* of July 7. Volunteers from churches and hospitals, from the Sisters of Charity and the Christian Commission of Philadelphia, from the Baltimore Fire Department, even the Adams Express Company arrived on the scene to help.

During July hundreds of bodies were dug up, placed in pine boxes, and shipped to grieving families. But it was an impossible task and a dangerous one, the workers insisted, fearing the sudden spread of unmanageable pestilence. By the end of July a military order was issued forbidding any more moving of bodies.

By then, too, the idea for some kind of permanent local resting place for the dead Union heroes was taking form. A Massachusetts committee that had been on the scene seeing to the state's dead sons proposed a national cemetery, and simultaneously a similar plan was put forth by a member of the Christian Commission. It was not long before an organized movement was under way, with Pennsylvania's David Wills as its leader. The governors of the other seventeen states involved speedily gave Wills their approval, and each state agreed to pay a prorated share (based on its overall population) of the cost of creating the cemetery.

Deciding that it was impractical to sort out the thousands of dead state by state, Wills first opted for "promiscuous" burial, but Massachusetts would not hear of it. By mid-August, therefore, when Wills had purchased the seventeen acres adjacent to Gettysburg's regular cemetery for $2,475.87, the character of the national commemoration had already been discussed and argued over. William Saunders, the landscape architect called in from Washington, was temporarily thrown off by the odd shape of the purchased land, but the acquisition of five additional acres gave him sufficient room to work. He chose a semicircular pattern of grave sites to fit the boot-shaped area. From a central point, the graves would fan out in a half-circle, each widening strip containing the fallen men of a different state, their bodies wrapped in army blankets and their heads resting upon pillows of wood shavings.

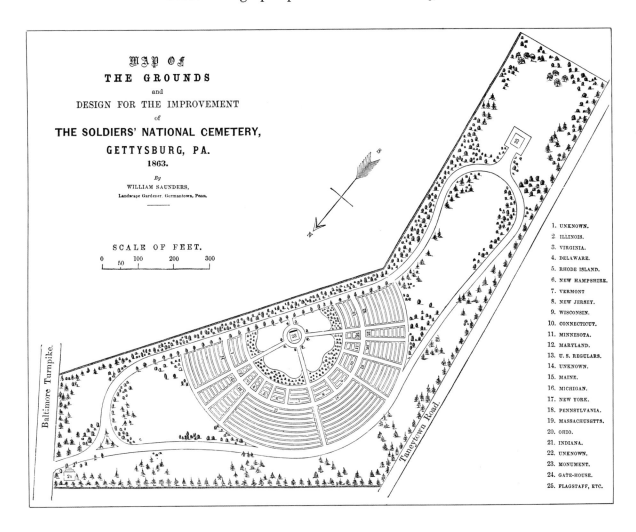

By mid-August Wills had also begun to consider what kind of dedication ceremony should take place once the cemetery was completed. On August 28 Governor Curtin was in Washington to see Lincoln. Their conversation that day probably provoked the letter Curtin wrote to Wills three days later. "The proper consecration of the grounds," it said, "should have early attention."

The most important event of the consecration would be the main oration; Wills and the governors of the participating states did not need to ruminate over the choice. No one could surpass the silver-tongued New Englander Edward Everett for cultured words and patriotic fervor. On the twenty-third of September Wills sent off a letter to Everett asking him to be the principal speaker at the Gettysburg exercises planned then to take place in exactly a month.

"I am . . . instructed by the governors of the different states interested in the project," Wills wrote, "to invite you cordially to join with them in ceremonies, and to deliver the oration for the occasion."

On the same day the Wills letter was mailed, Everett was visited at his home by the mayor of Boston, who proffered the invitation in person. Everett was pleased; he said he could find no way to refuse. But, he told Wills by return mail after the written invitation had arrived, the timetable was too hurried for adequate preparation. "I cannot safely name an earlier time," wrote Everett, "than the 19th of November. Should such a postponement of the day first proposed be admissible, it will give me great pleasure to accept the invitation."

The change of date that Everett proposed was acceptable; the nineteenth of November it would be.

"I . . . invite my fellow citizens in every part of the United States . . . to set apart and observe the last Thursday of November next, as a day of Thanksgiving and Praise to our beneficent Father who dwelleth in the

As far away as Hanover, bodies of the fallen were disinterred and taken to the new national cemetery at Gettysburg for reburial. Sixty bodies a day were all the workers could manage, but by the day of the ceremonies, 1,188 bodies had been moved and reburied. Of these, 582 could not be identified. Of the 606 that could, more than 100 were attributable to each of three states: Pennsylvania, New York, and Massachusetts. Samuel Weaver, the small man standing at the right, was one of those in charge of moving the Union dead. But on November 19 his occupation was less grisly: he and his brother Frank, from Baltimore, were on the scene with a fancy new camera wagon to photograph the proceedings.

Heavens." Having been prodded by magazine editor Sarah Josepha Hale, thus did Lincoln on October 3 establish Thanksgiving Day as a national holiday. The official statement was drafted for him by Secretary of State Seward.

A few days after that presidential proclamation, the grounds for the new national cemetery in Gettysburg were laid out, and by mid-

month bids were heard for the unappetizing job of exhuming the bodies of the Union dead that remained scattered throughout the Pennsylvania countryside, moving them to the site of the new cemetery, and reburying them. Thirty-four bids were received, ranging from $8.00 to $1.59 per body. Low bidder F. W. Biesecker was the winner, if one can call it that. Black laborers were hired to do the grisly work of digging up the decomposed remains and placing them in boxes with the aid of tongs. Tremendous care was taken to identify each body correctly; if a penciled headboard did not confirm the name, pockets were emptied, wallets searched, letters read, initials studied. Personal effects were then fastidiously put aside for later distribution to the appropriate family. Still, many bodies were unidentifiable and mistakes were made. Nothing as astonishing, though, as what had occurred after the battle at Cedar Mountain: a Maine couple who requested that the body of their son be returned home opened the casket upon delivery and were greeted by the remains of a Confederate soldier.

◦◦▸▭◂◦◦

Tradition has it that one day not long after the moving of the dead began in Gettysburg, Lincoln received one of the routine printed invitations that had been mailed off to all significant government and military officials asking them to attend the November 19 ceremonies. Many of these invitations were either preceded or followed by personal visits from members of the organizing committee or their associates. Since Governor Curtin saw Lincoln in Washington in late October, it was probably he who first proffered the invitation. Lincoln immediately let it be known that he accepted. This seemed to startle some of those in charge; no one had really expected that the President would leave the capital in wartime for anything but consultations with his generals or personal inspections of the battlefields. If the President was really going to attend, how could he not be invited to participate? How could he not be asked to speak?

The very thought of it made those in charge exceedingly nervous, claimed one authority. With an election year coming up, it was suspected that Lincoln would use the event for political purposes. Even more to the point, he was just not cut out for this kind of occasion. He could so easily be indelicate, or go into one of his embarrassing, off-the-cuff talks that made everybody wince. Would he treat the solemn day too lightly? And that newspaper story about the President riding through the Antietam battlefield . . .

Everybody knew that story wasn't true. Its mischievous author, Joseph Scovill, had admitted as much, calling it "only a joke." But yet . . . The President was reported to have laughed and joked with his friend and former Danville law partner Ward Hill Lamon as the two rode past burial parties in an open carriage. And hadn't that same story said that Lamon got out his banjo and started to play ribald songs? And that General George McClellan himself had to intervene right there in the carriage with a polite but icy "Not now, please!" to the President? And Lincoln — after that story was published, first in England and then in the always antagonistic *New York World* — hadn't Lincoln failed to refute it or even discuss it in any way? And hadn't he completely ignored the libelous verse the *World* published? —

> *Abe may crack his jolly jokes*
> *O'er bloody fields of stricken battle,*
> *While yet the ebbing life-tide smokes*
> *From men that die like butchered cattle.*

And now, on top of all this, Lincoln was helping to appoint this same man Lamon — who everybody knew drank too much, and was a brawler and a troublemaker, and spoke in a suspicious Southern drawl — to the position of chief marshal for the Gettysburg affair. David Wills had confirmed the appointment in a letter to Lamon written on October 30,

Ward Hill Lamon, the hard-living, fun-loving ex-Virginian whom Lincoln had befriended in Illinois, took it upon himself to guard the President in Washington whenever he had the time. Lincoln urged Lamon to be chief marshal of the ceremonies that would consecrate the national cemetery at Gettysburg. A champion wrestler who liked to sing and play his banjo, Lamon posed here in early 1861 with a few of the famous Brady props. The mourning band on his hat was in remembrance of his first wife, who died in 1859.

and Lincoln said he had told Lamon that "in view of his relationship to the government and to me . . . , he could not well decline." On November 4 Lamon "most cheerfully" accepted.

All this raised doubts and fears, supposedly, but still it was unthinkable not to ask the President to say something if he was going to make the trip. On November 2 Wills made the request official by writing Lincoln from Gettysburg. The President could not mistake what Wills was after. The letter was careful to point out that whatever Lincoln chose to say, his message had to be completely serious in nature, suitable to "kindle anew in the breasts of the Comrades of these brave dead" a confidence that the dead "are not forgotten by those highest in authority." As well as being serious and fitting, the letter emphasized, it had to be *short*. In fact, "a few appropriate remarks" would be just about right.

In the same mail, Wills sent a second, more personal letter to Lincoln. "As the hotels in our town will be crowded and in confusion at the time referred to in the extended invitation," it began, "I write to invite you to stop with me. . . . Governor Curtin and Honorable Edward Everett will be my guests at the time and if you come you will please join them at my house."

Although Everett had had almost two full months to prepare what he would say on the occasion, Lincoln now had hardly two weeks.

FOUR

IT could not have gone unnoticed by Lincoln that his invitation to speak at Gettysburg had been an afterthought, but it was not in his nature to feel slighted by such things. After he accepted, he began really thinking about what he would say at the dedication ceremonies. At first he didn't write anything down; instead in his mind he worked on the ideas he felt needed expressing and some of the words he knew he wanted to use.

It was funny how his mind seemed to go on working on the speech even when he wasn't awake, and certainly during the day when he was busy with other things; that is the way it had been with the farewell speech in Springfield and with his inaugural address. Now, back of every action, there was always Gettysburg. In the foreground were the details of presidential routine. There was a gold-headed cane to be accepted with an explanation of why he would value it forever. There were

7,500 men of the Invalid Corps to review in front of the White House. There were orders to give, like the one on November 11: "I personally wish Jacob R. Freese, of New Jersey, to be appointed a Colonel for a colored regiment — and this regardless of whether he can tell the exact shade of Julius Caesar's hair."

There were letters to write, such as the one dated November 9 to Judge Stephen T. Logan back in Springfield suggesting that he come east to the Gettysburg dedication. "It will be an interesting ceremony and I shall be very glad to see you." The reason for the President's letter was not that he was lonely for his old friend and former law partner, however, but rather to suggest persuasively that the judge bring with him his daughter Sally, the wife of Hill Lamon. Having spent all summer in Illinois visiting her parents, she had now summoned her husband: if he did not come this minute and escort her back to Washington, then he need never come.

It was a crisis — but the President was anxious to have Lamon stay in Washington and carry out the duties given him as marshal of the District of Columbia: to be chief marshal of the day at Gettysburg. In that position Lamon would be able to introduce his friend Lincoln when the President stood up to speak. So close was the two men's relationship that this meant a great deal to them. The plan worked, and Sally was soon happily on her way east with the judge.

As Lincoln began to jot down ideas for the speech, what began to develop had a biblical ring to it — not unexpectedly, since the Bible had been his chief reading during childhood. In fact, it still was. The President spent time alone each morning in the family library reading Bible passages, just before going down the hall to begin the day in his office.

A pair of social engagements served as counterpoint to the alchemy of oratorical composition. On November 9, two days after the public had been asked to the Gettysburg exercises through the nation's newspapers, Lincoln went to the performance at Ford's Theater and sat in the box he regularly occupied in the second tier to the right, a curtained hideaway of lush red satin and brocade — perfect for reflecting on a cemetery while the eyes were watching the stage. That evening John Wilkes Booth was playing in *The Marble Heart*, portraying a Greek sculptor whose statues come to life. An extraordinarily handsome figure he was, in his antique costume, with those wild black curls and strange, smoldering black eyes. Before the curtain went up, the statues — three actresses in white tights and wigs, standing on a pedestal and almost asphyxiated by a heavy dusting of white powder — had the thrill of being arranged in their poses by the sculptor-actor himself. The high point of the play came at the pretty sight of three "marble" arms moving with one accord to point at their astonished creator.

The sole other respite for Lincoln was the fashionable wedding on November 12 of Kate Chase. The President was obliged to attend, because the bride was the daughter of his secretary of the treasury. But he would go alone, for Mary Lincoln detested Kate. Mrs. Lincoln had often instructed her husband not to talk to the bewitching Miss C. at receptions — she was deceitful. Mary Lincoln did not approve of the President flirting with silly women. "But Mother," he would say mildly, "I insist that I must talk with somebody. I can't stand around like a simpleton and say nothing." This evening, bearing a small fan to add to the record $100,000 worth of gifts the bride received, he went to offer his good wishes to the belle of Washington — the girl with the tiniest waist in the capital city — Kate of the outrageous little tilted nose that wrinkled so deliciously. Lincoln mingled with the wedding guests, got a general impression of lights and colorful uniforms and the buzz of animated voices, and congratulated the bridegroom — wealthy, handsome William Sprague, former governor of Rhode Island, who had resigned to represent his state in the Senate. The President was home again in a matter of minutes, having flirted not at all. Seven more days to the Gettysburg ceremony, but he must try to keep his anxiety over exactly

Six days before leaving for Gettysburg, Lincoln attended the wedding of one of his favorites: Kate Chase — the reigning belle of Washington, daughter of the secretary of the treasury, and a constant irritant to Mary Lincoln because of her beauty, her vivacious personality, and her desire to outshine the President's wife.

what to say there within bounds. His long annual message to Congress had to be ready for delivery on December 8, nineteen days after the cemetery consecration.

On Thursday, the twelfth of November (the same day as the Chase wedding), Ward Hill Lamon, accompanied by Benjamin B. French, the chief marshal's choice as his top aide, started out by rail for Gettysburg at six-thirty in the morning. Only a week before the big day, they were on their way to check out preparations for the ceremonies. French, the sixty-three-year-old New Hampshire–reared commissioner of public buildings, was a Washington fixture — quiet, self-effacing, always the gentleman. One of his duties was to introduce Mary Lincoln at White House receptions — even though he was high on the First Lady's list of unpopular people.

Lamon was known as the President's self-appointed bodyguard and had even gone so far as to sleep on the floor outside Lincoln's White House room in order to protect him. He also had been accused of using his friendship with Lincoln to his special advantage — in particular, to exploit inside knowledge of commodity transactions. Lincoln had installed his friend as marshal of the District of Columbia over the protests of certain members of Congress and of the Supreme Court, who did not want an outsider filling the post. But when Lamon wrote the President a wrathful note demanding that he reject a bill, already passed by both houses of Congress, that would reduce by one-half the fees the marshal got for arrests, captures, and warrants, Lincoln merely wrote at the bottom of the letter, "I regret this, but I cannot veto a bill of this character."

Lincoln stuck by Lamon, however, when the marshal's method of arrest became so extreme one night that he almost killed a man. "Hereafter," said Lincoln, "when you have occasion to strike a man, don't hit him with your fist; strike him with a club or crowbar or something that won't kill him."

On the sixth of January of this very year, the President had given Hill Lamon a gold Tiffany watch for his thirty-fifth birthday. It was a curious friendship: the quiet man with the obsession for the right words and for finding the right rhythm and order for them — and who, his wife said, had a sort of poetry in his soul; and the six-foot-two-inch, red-blooded, elegant yet course former Virginian who daily blustered about his devotion to Lincoln and the sacrifices he was making to serve him.

Arriving at Gettysburg, Lamon and French checked in at the Eagle Hotel before drawing up the final program for November 19 in David Wills's office. That night, back at the Eagle, French did some composing.

"Instead of sleeping," he wrote in his diary he filled with a lifetime's astute but often fussy observations, "I composed some rhymes for the celebration. Mr. Wills had told us, during the evening, that he had endeavored to get Longfellow, and Bryant, and Whittier . . . to write something, who all declined. So my muse volunteered. I arose early . . . and reduced my thoughts of the night to writing and gave a copy to Mr. Wills, and another to Col. Lamon. Perhaps it will be used — perhaps not. I did my best."

Frost had touched the capital as winter showed its first real signs. Brisk November winds had stripped the trees of their autumn foliage. Thin skims of ice formed on puddles overnight and a few flakes of snow shook down from heavy skies. Friday the thirteenth brought a rain shower late in the afternoon and more rain into the night. When the Gettysburg advance party returned the following evening, it was met by thunder rolling over the capital, sharp streaks of lightning, and more heavy rain, which lasted well into Sunday morning. That evening, Lamon held a meeting of the large Washington contingent of his Gettysburg aides.

When all the orders and information had been given out, departure times were discussed and fixed upon. Now the always cautious French vainly tried to persuade the group not to leave as late as the 3:00 P.M. train Tuesday. "If you postpone going until that time," he told the assemblage, "you'll probably be out all night." They ignored his advice, and French turned out to be right.

As for Lincoln, his daily routine continued even though Gettysburg and his "few appropriate remarks" were never far out of his mind. It was a wonder that the President could do any thinking at all during the work-day. After rising early and taking breakfast in the upstairs family dining room — an egg, a piece of toast, a cup of coffee — Lincoln opened the folding doors that cut off the White House living area from the official offices and, on appointed days, was swiftly swamped by office seekers, favor askers, and just plain visitors who thought it their due to meet him and who were already waiting their turns. Men wanting official posts of one kind or another were most in evidence at the beginning of Lincoln's administration; he heard each one out, took his papers, and either sent him on his way or to the proper agency or authority. Now, two and a half years later, the pardon seekers were in the majority.

Lincoln met with anyone seeking an audience — from politicians and financiers, writers, ministers, scientists, powerful newspaper editors, inventors, artists, and actors, to the most humble and least prepossessing farmer or widow. That was part of the job, Lincoln felt — to be available to the people, to actually meet with them in his office, to take each by the hand, personally listen to their problems or requests, and to help them whenever he could. Along with all his other duties, this kind of personal presidency sapped Lincoln's strength — and wasted a lot of his precious time as well. At least, "wasted" was what some of his associates called it; Lincoln didn't. Advance appointments were not necessary: just gain entrance at the main door of the White House — and that was easy if you weren't carrying a rifle or a club — go up the wide stairs to the second floor, and have a seat in the anteroom. Help fill, as Secretary Seward put it, "the grounds, hallways, stairways, closets" making "ingress and egress difficult." Join, as the famous "eye-witness" reporter George Alfred Townsend called them, the "duns and loiterers, contract hunters and seekers for commissions, garrulous parents on paltry errands, toadies without measure and talkers without conscience." Lincoln put it differently. "They don't want much," he said. "They get but little, and I must see them." He called the process "the only link or cord which connects the people with the governing power; and, however unprofitable much of it is, it must be kept up."

Those waiting might even be treated to the sight of Lincoln escaping to his meager lunch of a biscuit and a glass of milk or, in the summer, an apple or a bunch of grapes. For the President had ordered a structural addition when he moved into the White House and saw the lay of the working area. A narrow passageway was built that would allow him to get from his office right through the anteroom to the family library without being seen. Or so he thought. The carpenters assigned to the job did not know that Lincoln was eight inches taller than the average man of the day, so the walls of their passageway did not extend much higher than six feet. Lincoln's supposedly invisible departures from his office were therefore usually marked by the humorous sight of the top of his head bobbing above the partition as he moved across the crowded anteroom.

Lincoln's office was not only the place where the President met "the people." It also acted as the center of American government, where bills were signed, ambassadors greeted, senators and congressmen heard out; where presidential speeches were written; where generals and admirals congregated to report on the progress of the war; where cabinet meetings took place.

A messenger sat at the door to the office to bring in cards or names of visitors, who were then given treatment in the order of their rank. Cabinet members were seen immediately, and so were high military officers. The vice-president outranked senators and members of the House, who often arrived early — eight or nine in the morning — presenting their cards and waiting their turns either in the anteroom or in the hallway itself (where Lincoln might get a glimpse of them, they hoped, when the door opened). To those waiting outside, the ringing laugh of the President within could make jaws freeze, teeth clench; it seemed to many that he was wasting time inside, telling jokes and laughing away when he should have been hurrying through his business.

Lincoln's office was a long, high room with dark green wallpaper punctuated by gold star-patterns and intersecting diagonals. The doors were of imitation mahogany, the carpet dark green with crossbars and buff diamond-shaped figures. A long oak table covered with a heavy cloth and surrounded by rickety oak chairs used at cabinet meetings sat in the middle of the room. Lit by a globed chandelier that hung from the ceiling just above it, this central table was always the resting place for a clutter of letters and orders, the latest newspapers, rolled-up maps, designs for new inventions, references from office seekers, and anything else that might have found its way into the inner sanctum and been laid aside for the time being by the President.

As the piles of job applications grew and became more unwieldly, Lincoln's patience sometimes diminished, but seldom his sense of humor. Once two very loud contenders for the same office brought such loads of paper to prove their respective worths that Lincoln finally threw up his hands and called for a set of scales. With these he proceeded to weigh the sheaves each applicant had brought. One outweighed the other by three-quarters of a pound — and that man got the job.

John Hay, the President's secretary, noted a time when Lincoln's calm evaporated. On a hot summer afternoon, a private in the army

This photograph of Lincoln — taken by one of Brady's photographers at the request of the artist Francis B. Carpenter, who wanted it to paint from — shows a few details of the President's office. At the left is his chair. In the background, a high desk supporting filing slots and a row of books blocks off the door leading to the route used by Lincoln early in his presidency to escape crowds of visitors. The table next to the President accommodated cabinet meetings. At the far right is the edge of the fireplace with its marble mantelpiece.

somehow got into Lincoln's office and began stating his case over and over again, calling on the President to adjudicate it. Lincoln finally exploded. "Now, my man, go away! I cannot attend to all these details. I could as easily bail out the Potomac with a spoon." On another rare occasion of anger, Lincoln actually threw a particularly objectionable officer out of his office by the coat collar. "Sir," he said through pursed lips, "I give you fair warning never to show yourself in this room again. I can bear censure, but not insult."

On the office wall to the left of the door to the great hall, above a sofa and two armchairs, were two or three map frames, from which hung unfurled military maps with tracings upon them. Colored pushpins designated different armies, and Lincoln studiously moved them about when military campaigns were under way.

On the opposite wall was a large marble fireplace with old-fashioned brass andirons and a high brass fender. On its marble mantel sat a small pendulum clock encased in a dome of glass. Over the mantel hung the only picture in the room, a painting of Andrew Jackson that Lincoln had taken a fancy to in his early White House days; his wife, noting her husband's admiration for the work, had had it cleaned and repaired, and the frame regilded and revarnished for him. Lincoln would add a second picture later — a photograph of John Bright, the British statesman who believed in "the people" much the same way Lincoln did, and who corresponded with the President frequently.

At the far end of the room, two high, curtained windows, one on each side, looked southward toward the White House lawn and shrubbery, with the stump of the as-yet-unfinished Washington Monument behind them. Beyond lay the Potomac and the rolling Virginia hills, which Lincoln often gazed at through the powerful telescope he kept close at hand.

At the right-hand window was the President's personal armchair. Settled onto its black horsehair upholstery, he could either face out the window or swing around to his left, to a low desk where he did his writing and kept a pile of little blank cards he used for messages. To his right, against the south wall and between the windows, was a high postmaster's bureau with wooden doors that concealed pigeonholes crammed with notes and letters. The pigeonholes were marked in alphabetical order, but a few important and prolific letter-writers had slots all their own — among them, Horace Greeley and several generals. Why not a letter-book? Lincoln was asked. "A letter-book might be easily stolen and carried off," the President replied, "but that stock of filed letters would be a back-load."

Against the west wall was another desk, high enough to write upon while standing, and on top of this were more cubbyholes and a row of books, including the Bible, the statutes of the United States, a copy of the complete Shakespeare, and *Whiting's War Powers*. Close to Lincoln's chair dangled a bell cord that would summon one of his aides.

And that was all. That was the extent of the immediate facilities Lincoln had for running the country. He had no personal library, nor anyone who could take shorthand. He kept no diary. His secretaries threw up their hands over his lack of organization, but whenever they tried to organize him, it never worked. Lincoln noted things he wanted to remember on cards and filed them in nooks and crannies. On the postmaster's bureau was a special pile of papers on which the President tossed items he thought he might need. "When you can't find it anywhere else," Lincoln said, referring to this disarrayed cache of documents, "look in this!"

Lincoln's mind was a mystery. How it worked was his own private secret. It worked best when he was comfortable. Back in Springfield, seated in his law office, he sometimes threw a leg up onto another chair for better concentration. Or at home in Illinois he might assume a position on the floor, propped up against a pillow and the back of an overturned chair. In Washington he was usually careful to be more formal.

Sometimes, after reading, he would lie down and shut his eyes to better let the ideas sink in. Often his mind would drift off from what was going on around him. He had a way of coming back to reality by suddenly quoting a few lines of poetry out of the blue — it took other people's minds off what he might really have been thinking about. Sometimes his fits of abstraction were so deep, only his name repeated over and over would break the spell. He would shake his head and laugh and say that his "wits had gone wool-gathering."

Lincoln relentlessly analyzed everything. "He would stop in the street and study a machine," said his law partner William Herndon.

He would whittle things to a point and then count the numberless inclined planes and their pitch making the point. Mastering and defining this, he would cut that point back and get a broad transverse section of his pine stick and peel and define that. Clocks, omnibuses, and language, paddlewheels and idioms never escaped his observation and analysis. Before he could form an idea of anything, before he expressed his opinion, he must know it in origin and history, in substance and quality, in magnitude and gravity. He must know his subject inside and outside, upside and downside.

Logic and reason — he had said it himself back in 1838 — "cold, calculating, unimpassioned reason" was part of his secret. And complete lack of interest in the normal, everyday rules of human conduct was another. "He did not care for forms, ways, methods," said Herndon, ". . . nor did he manifest an intense interest in any individual man — the dollar, property, rank, order, manners, or similar things."

These traits — logic and reason, and a disregard for the rules — came through in Lincoln's writings, which he helped himself to accomplish through a variety of small rituals: by submerging himself in hard thinking while he ate his meals — never mentioning whether what had been put before him was good, bad, or indifferent; by gnawing on the end of his pen or pencil as he paused to think between sentences, leaving chewed wood behind as he composed; by dipping his pen in the inkwell, then waiting, thinking, waiting some more, until the pen had dried and he started dipping once again; by turning to the dictionary, searching through it, and complaining to his secretaries that he could not find the words to express exactly what he had in mind. But whatever his tactics for thought, however he created his memorable words, Lincoln did not assist his biographers by talking or writing about the process that went on in his mind while writing.

William C. Herndon, a former law partner of Lincoln's, wrote some of the most evocative descriptions of him.

Nor did he help them with much biographical detail of any kind. The course of Lincoln's life up until the moment he assumed the presidency was known to all while he was in office, but without the infinite variety of colorful detail that would come later. The human-interest tidbits that would have quickened the nation's heart and fleshed out the classic circumstances of the self-educated boy who became President were absent because Lincoln insisted that official descriptions of him be modest and not go much beyond the spare material he had provided. "There is no romance, nor is there anything heroic in my early life," he told a frustrated campaign biographer. "The story of my life can be condensed into one line, and that line you can find in Gray's Elegy, 'the short and simple annals of the poor.' This is all you or anyone can make out of me or my early life."

Actually, Lincoln simply did not believe that personal matters such as the details of his poverty-shadowed childhood were of interest. His severe dictum was that "history is not history unless it is the truth," and its narrow outlook eliminated from his first biographies not only the embroidery he hoped to avoid but some fascinating truth as well. To follow Lincoln, to try to understand his mind during the years of his presidency, people had to study his documents and letters and speeches, largely through the newspapers. It was not ideal, but there lay the answer to how his mind worked when he wrote — within his writings themselves.

Sometime between the day he accepted David Wills's invitation to speak at Gettysburg and the time of his departure from Washington for the ceremonies two weeks later, Lincoln put on paper at least some of the speech he would make. Twice during those days he visited the photographic gallery of Alexander Gardner and his brother James, who were working hard on their *Photographic Incidents of the War*, making careful prints of the harrowing scenes they had taken after the battle at

Twice before leaving for Gettysburg — on two successive Sundays — Lincoln went to Alexander and James Gardner's gallery at the intersection of Pennsylvania and Seventh to have his picture taken.

Gettysburg in July. So hectic was their schedule that they would not apply for copyrights to these war pictures until the very last day of the year.

The portraits taken of Lincoln during these two visits to the Gardner studio give a clear and permanent picture of just what he looked like during the time his Gettysburg words were taking form. On November 8, a cloudy morning that cleared by noon, Lincoln posed with his secretaries John Nicolay and John Hay; a brooding, distant picture shows a large-jawed, seated Lincoln, with the much smaller Nicolay (recently returned

On November 8 Lincoln posed with his two personal secretaries, John Nicolay (seated) and John Hay.

from a recuperative trip to the Rocky Mountains) awkwardly seated to his right, and the debonair Hay standing to the President's left, one hand on hip, the other on the back of Lincoln's chair. "Nico and I immortalized ourselves by having ourselves done in a group with the Prest.," John Hay wrote in his diary that day.

Then, exactly a week later, on November 15 — again on Sunday, so as not to disrupt the photographers' normal business — Lincoln sat for the Gardners and at least four exposures were made. In the two full-length seated poses, an envelope lay on the table beside Lincoln's resting right hand. Noah Brooks, a discerning newspaperman who had become close to Lincoln and was later scheduled to take the place of Nicolay and Hay as the President's private secretary, was a spectator at the sitting and long afterward claimed that the envelope contained Edward Everett's Gettysburg speech, thoughtfully sent to Lincoln by its author so that the President wouldn't repeat anything that the main orator was planning to say. Although there is doubt that Everett's especially printed speech could have arrived in Washington that early, Brooks quoted Lincoln on his own progress. Lincoln, Brooks said, was gratified that Everett had taken the trouble to send his speech along so that there would be no overlap, but Everett need not have worried. His own offering, Lincoln said, was going to be "short, short, short." Was it written yet? "Well, not exactly written, not finished anyway."

Six o'clock was dinner time at the White House; the President would eat anything put in front of him as long as it wasn't too fancy. Even though Mary Lincoln had set a stingy table back in Springfield, still her husband's appetite had not always been as spare and uninterested as it was now. Back then, he used to say he could gobble up corn cakes just as fast as any two women could make them. But now he ate mechanically, getting little pleasure out of taste or texture. He drank nothing but water,

On November 15 newsman Noah Brooks (at right) accompanied his friend the President to the Gardner gallery. Many years later Brooks claimed that in the pictures taken that day, such as the one at left, the envelope beside Lincoln's right hand contained a copy of the speech Edward Everett planned to make at Gettysburg four days later. "We did not have to wait long between the sittings," wrote Brooks, "and the President, having taken out the envelope and laid it on a little table at his elbow, became so engaged in talk that he failed to open it while we were at the studio." Some experts think that this picture actually was taken a week earlier, on November 8 — which would make it chronologically impossible for the envelope to have contained advance printer's proof of Everett's speech. Even if the photograph was indeed taken on the fifteenth, as has long been believed, the letter containing Everett's printed speech probably could not yet have reached the President.

although occasionally, when his stomach was bothering him, he would take a glass of ale or even champagne as a tonic. When guests were present and wine was served, he merely touched some to his lips to be polite. Sometimes he asked a friend to take potluck with him, but usually the family dined alone. When his wife was away, Lincoln browsed around at dinner, pacing about and finally taking his food upstairs on a tray; then he might forget about it completely after picking up his pen.

But mostly Lincoln wrote in his office, during the daytime hours. He wrote slowly, lost in thought, his eyes sometimes drifting to the window. A secretary might interrupt him with a pile of papers to sign; he did it almost by rote, never really allowing his mind to leave the subject he was writing about. And if he did take his eyes from the page and turn his attention to another matter, he could return to what he had been working on an hour later and pick up exactly where he left off, without rereading what he had already put down.

"My mind," said Lincoln, "is like a piece of steel — very hard to scratch anything on it, almost impossible after you get it there to rub it out."

Many remarked on Lincoln's extraordinary memory, saying he could repeat whatever he read almost word for word and that events in his mind were always associated with dates. It is surprising that with such a memory Lincoln was not more of a plagiarist. He did not need to be — he was overflowing with his own thoughts and arrangements of words — but he did borrow without qualm, especially when what he was borrowing seemed to strike the perfect tone. From George Washington he took "our common country" and "I bid you an affectionate farewell," and he slightly changed old Governor Ninian Edwards's words "I would far rather fall nobly than rise meanly" to "we shall nobly save or meanly lose the last best hope of earth." The Declaration's "all men are created equal" had been used before by Lincoln in his Henry Clay eulogy. And the use, in various forms, of the three prepositions — *of* the people, *by* the people, *for* the people — has been attributed to at least twelve men, including Patrick Henry and Daniel Webster. Probably the most likely source was Theodore Parker, the abolitionist minister from Massachusetts whose lectures and sermons had been printed and were called to Lincoln's attention by his law partner William Herndon. "Democracy is self-government," Parker had said, "over all the people, for all the people, by all the people."

It didn't matter; it was the important things Lincoln had to say that made the difference. What wasn't important, he learned, had better be left unsaid, for Lincoln was helpless at speaking or writing when he had nothing to say. To be effective he had to be prepared, but prepared in the right way. For he also learned that he was poor in setting down his thoughts in the form of lectures, that he was no poet, and that he was not funny on the printed page.

Even though he couldn't write poetry well, Lincoln dearly loved it and was deeply moved by it. When he himself had tried to versify, as he used to do now and again, the roses he wrote about didn't fade or wither — they rotted; and his long poems, about a bear hunt and an old friend who became insane, were singsong doggerel.

Longfellow's two lines

> *Our hearts, our hopes, our prayers, our tears,*
> *Our faith triumphant o'er our fears,*

made Lincoln cry and reflect, "It's a wonderful gift to be able to stir men like that." He tried once to recite from Oliver Wendell Holmes's "Lexington" the lines

> *Green be the graves where her martyrs are lying!*
> *Shroudless and tombless they sunk to their rest,*

and couldn't get through them for sobbing.

He liked sad poems about death and how rapidly it can snatch one away.

He admired Holmes's "Last Leaf" and said that for "pure pathos" he thought "there is nothing finer in the English language than those six lines" in particular from it:

> *The mossy marbles rest*
> *On the lips that he has prest*
>   *In their bloom,*
> *And the names he loved to hear*
> *Have been carved for many a year*
>   *On the tomb.*

His absolute, all-time favorite poem was by the Scottish poet William Knox.

> *Oh, why should the spirit of mortal be proud?*
> *Like a swift-flitting meteor, a fast-flying cloud,*
> *A flash of the lightning, a break of the wave,*
> *He passeth from life to his rest in the grave.*
>
> · · · · · · · · · · · ·
>
> *'Tis the wink of an eye; 'tis the draught of a breath*
> *From the blossom of health to the paleness of death,*
> *From the gilded saloon to the bier and the shroud;*
> *Oh, why should the spirit of mortal be proud?*

Considering his somber poetic tastes, it seems odd that Lincoln was so noted as a teller of funny stories — all someone else's originally, though he split people's sides retelling them. But when he tried to devise humor himself on the written page, it came out weak and mild.

The President read from the works of the humorist Petroleum V. Nasby, found all of them convulsing, and even expressed his envy. "For the genius to write these things," he said, "I would gladly give up my office."

Lincoln decided early that in his address at Gettysburg he would mention not a single person. Nor would he describe the battle or the scene. It would have been easy to tell how decisive the fighting at Gettysburg had been, or just where in the war the country stood at that very moment. No, instead of being detailed and specific, Lincoln had decided to deal with larger issues. And his language would be lofty and classical in its ring and tone; there would be none of his now famous and colorful animal analogies for critics to jump on and use as examples of how the President was making light of the occasion.

As early as the famous debates of 1858, Lincoln was using animal imagery, calling his opponent Stephen A. Douglas a toothless lion, a bear that was so hard pressed she was willing to drop her cub to make her own escape, and a cuttlefish that throws out "a dark fluid which makes the water so dark the enemy cannot see it; and thus it escapes." (The wording describing cuttlefish in a copy of *Animated Nature* owned by a neighbor and often studied intently by Lincoln ends "by which the waters are totally darkened and then it escapes.")

But merely calling people animals was a simple business, and in Washington Lincoln devised something more complicated metaphorically and rather unusual in the leader of a nation. As Charles Sumner remarked, Lincoln's ideas walked along in pairs, like animals entering the ark. The President did not say, "I will pardon these prisoners"; he said, "I will turn out the flock" or "open the gates, let down the bars, scare them off." He did not say, "I will never be able to find enough places for these office seekers"; he said, "There are too many pigs for the tits."

General Halleck was given a warning: "The hen is the wisest of all animal creation, because she never cackles till the egg is laid." He thought of General John Pope as an ox. "Pope went all night until one day we geed him when we ought to have hawed him." The part of the divided country that Lincoln was President of had turned out, he said, to be an elephant. "If I can only keep my end of the animal pointed in the right direction, I will get through this infernal jungle."

Perhaps Lincoln was beginning to feel the emotion he would express at Gettysburg when this detail from another Gardner portrait was exposed.

Though the Emancipation Proclamation was signed, slavery was not dead — no, Lincoln exclaimed, it was a whale. "We have at last got the harpoon into the monster, but we must now look how we steer, or with one flop of his tail, he will send us all into eternity." To General Joseph Hooker: "If the head of Lee's army is at Martinsburg and the tail of it on the plank road between Fredericksburg and Chancellorsville, the animal must be very thin somewhere. Could you not break him?" To General Halleck again: "The rebellion can only eke out a short and feeble existence, as an animal sometimes may with a thorn in its vitals." And, most recently, to General Meade after Gettysburg: "But Meade, it seems to me you shooed the geese over the river."

It was a language that had originated out of Lincoln's forest boyhood, from the stables and barnyards and chicken coops that had been so much a part of his life, and from his curiosity about the beasts of the sea and of Africa that he read about and marveled over. But it was not the kind of language he envisioned using at the Gettysburg dedication.

The words Lincoln finally chose to use (or ones close to them) fitted on a page or two. Fearing a disaster, or afraid of building up too great an expectation, the President seemed not to want to admit that his speech was down on paper at all. Three days before departure he had told Noah Brooks that the speech was "not finished anyway." Only a day before leaving, Lincoln said to Attorney General James Speed that it was only half-written. He had shown it to Simon Cameron, orginally his secretary of war. "It was written," Cameron said, "with a lead pencil on commercial notepaper."

And the President had told his friend Hill Lamon that the writing was not going smoothly. Lamon recalled that Lincoln then took off his hat — which he regularly used as a desk drawer, tucking important papers beneath the inner rim — and withdrew a single piece of foolscap with writing upon it in the President's own hand. Lincoln made Lamon aware that he felt displeasure with the words he was about to read to him. "Hill, there is what I have written for Gettysburg tomorrow," Lamon remembered Lincoln saying. "It does not suit me, but I have not time for anything more." Then he read the words aloud.

When Lincoln finished, he paused, waiting for his friend to respond. But by his silence Lamon let Lincoln know that he wasn't impressed. That kind of lofty language, those kind of high-blown thoughts, had gone right over the chief marshal's head.

FIVE

HAVING been named by Secretary of War Stanton himself to be Lincoln's personal escort for the trip, Provost Marshal General James B. Fry arrived at the White House at eleven-thirty. The carriage was waiting; the President was not. The doctor had come, hovered over the sick boy, and issued bad news. Mrs. Lincoln, still dressed in black following the death of her beloved Willie a year and a half ago, was beside herself. The President had made his decision: he would go.

General Fry urged him to hurry. "There is no time to lose," he told Lincoln. Only the day before, Lincoln himself had rejected Stanton's plan for the President to make the journey to Gettysburg and back to Washington all in one day. "I do not like this arrangement," Lincoln had advised him. "I do not wish to so go that by the slightest accident we fail entirely, and, at the best, the whole to be a mere breathless running of the gauntlet."

Now not a train schedule but a family illness was threatening Lincoln's speaking appointment in Gettysburg.

Again the general urged the President to hurry, and soon they were clattering toward the station, carriage wheels spinning in a whir to make up for lost time — but not before Lincoln had responded to Fry with one of his favorite stories. It was about the man, the President said, who had been sentenced to hang. On the way to the gallows this condemned murderer was struck by all the excitement around him as crowds surged ahead to get to the site for a good view of the execution. "Boys, you needn't be in such a hurry," he called out to them. "There won't be any fun until I get there."

It was a typical Lincoln story, heard somewhere long ago, stored somewhere in his voluminous memory to use in a situation like this. And it was indicative of the odd way the President often sprang his humorous tales when solemnity seemed to be in order. It was one of the characteristics that surprised and befuddled many who came in contact with him — that way he had of making light of things when adversity was close by, and then even leaning over and slapping his knee and laughing his head off as if he'd never heard his own story before. It was the kind of behavior that frightened people who wanted Lincoln to participate in serious occasions. And for this reason he had almost deliberately been excluded from the Gettysburg ceremony.

When Lincoln arrived at the train station and stepped from his carriage, he was ushered to the tracks by a lieutenant, a sergeant, and ten privates from the Invalid Corps. It was not hard for him to tell which train had been appointed to do the honors. A four-coach special awaited him, its locomotive decked out with silk streamers and red-white-and-blue bunting. The jam around its cars — the invited guests, the saluting soldiers, the bustling train officials, the excited travelers to other points who had

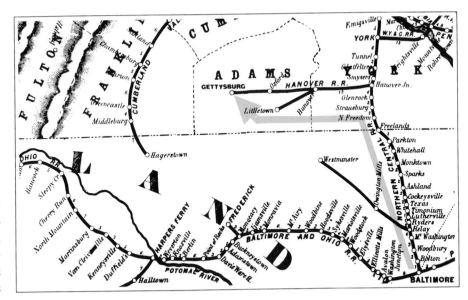

An 1863 railroad map showing the route Lincoln's train took from Baltimore to Gettysburg via Hanover Junction

been drawn from the waiting room in hopes of catching a glimpse of the President — all this told him to heed the urgings of chief conductor John W. Showacre, swing himself aboard, and let the journey get under way. It speedily did, only ten minutes late, with a great deal of hissing from the engine, eruptions of white steam, the clang of the bell, the hoot of the whistle, the clouds of spark-filled smoke that belched forth from the smokestack, the grinding of wheel against track. Inside the coaches, Lincoln and his special traveling companions were settling down for the trip of about 120 miles — nearly twice the direct distance to Gettysburg, over a roadbed that would give their teeth a good rattle and make them hold on to their seats for dear life.

The route to Gettysburg, a town only eight miles north of the Mason-Dixon line, had been carefully planned by the War Department. It called for a 1¼-hour run to Baltimore, a switch of tracks, continuing northward through Woodbury, Ryders, Timonium, Cockeysville, Sparks, and Monktown on the Northern Central, passing from Maryland into Pennsylvania at Freelands, and turning due west at Hanover Junction for the final thirty miles to Gettysburg. From July 9 to August 1, over

Almost any chair was too small for him, and his knees would stick up like prongs.

fifteen thousand wounded had been transported east over the tracks of this final run.

For the sake of the President, the Baltimore & Ohio Railroad had temporarily walled off the last third of the car that brought up the rear of the train, a special coach normally used by the railroad's board of directors. Chairs were set along the walls of the temporary room, and on one of them sat Lincoln, pale and a bit grim. Was he coming down with something? He had said as much to his secretaries that morning, but Tad's illness had taken all the attention. Now he seemed very thin and forlorn in his long-coated black suit. The chair was too small for him, as well — too low, as most chairs were — and because of it his knees stuck up about his waist like prongs.

He was a giant for his day — six feet, four inches — and all his life he had used that marvelous height to his advantage, realizing the commanding presence it gave him. He had seen its effects on crowds in the debates with five-foot-four-inch Stephen Douglas. He was exceedingly proud of his height and had a hobby of measuring himself, back to back, with any other tall man who came along. A critical press accused him of unseemly conduct, pointing out that the first thing he did on receiving in his Springfield home the committee bringing him notification of his nomination for the presidency was to suggest measuring himself against the highest member of the group. He measured, they wrote, at every station stop across the country on his way to Washington, picking some bean-pole yokel from out of the crowd. He continued his pastime at White House receptions and on trips to the front, and even interrupted important conferences with "Let's have a try if you can overtop me."

Growing up, Lincoln had also used to advantage the great, sinewy strength that went with his length, whacking axes farther into logs than anyone else, wrestling all comers to their backs, lifting enormous hogs for market, winning footraces — he could go a record forty-one feet in three hops.

OPPOSITE: *In October of 1862 Lincoln visited General George B. McClellan (sixth from left) at his headquarters at Antietam, Maryland. Alexander Gardner was there, and the pictures he took show Lincoln's great height. In this picture, Lincoln towered over every officer present, even though his knee was bent and he stooped slightly as he leaned on the back of a chair.*

RIGHT: *This image shows Lincoln a head higher than General John A. McClernand (at right) and detective Allan Pinkerton, who called himself Major E. J. Allen when doing wartime secret service.*

The great, hard, muscular hands of Lincoln's frontier youth had slowly changed as the focus of his life had changed from the physical to things of the mind. Now those hands were graceful, with long, sensitive fingers, and they lay in his lap in repose like sculptured models, thumbs just touching the tops of the fingers. His feet were enormous — long and narrow with exaggerated big toes; it took size-14 shoes to encase them.

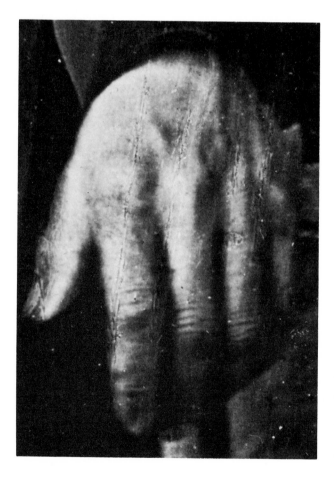

LEFT & OPPOSITE: *The muscular, wood-chopper's hands of Lincoln's forest and barnyard youth slowly thinned, grew graceful, as he left the physical behind and turned more and more toward pursuits of the mind.*

Lincoln's looks were continually changing. There was so much tightening and loosening of facial muscles, so many different kinds of flashes to his blue-gray eyes, so many sudden turns of mood, that no description or recollection or rendition of his looks was ever completely correct. "Angular," they called him. "Shriveled." "Queer-looking." Some came right out and said it: "ugly" — hawk-nosed, sallow-skinned, ears

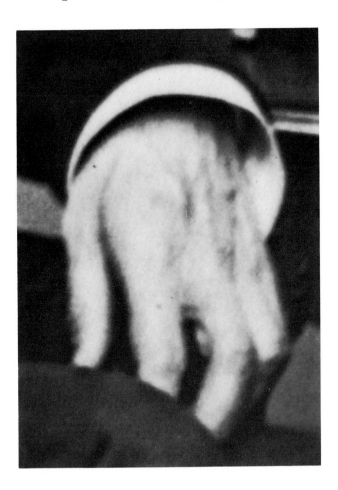

big as flapjacks, drooping lip. And Lincoln didn't do much to change these opinions. "I was accosted by a stranger" — he loved telling the story — "who said, 'Excuse me, sir, I have an article in my possession which belongs to you!' 'How is that?' I asked considerably astonished. The stranger took a jackknife from his pocket. 'This knife,' he said, 'was placed in my hands some years ago, with the injunction that I was to keep it until I found a man uglier than myself. I have to say, sir, that I think you are fairly entitled to the property.'"

Actually, it was a sad face, with deep wrinkles, but one that became radiant when an idea struck the mind behind. The left eye wandered. Whiskers, grown in the four months before he came to Washington to serve as President, made him seem older. So did the forty pounds he had lost between his nomination and his departure from Springfield. A fresh haircut could take years off him. His facial structure was hard, lean, bony. His skin was like leather. As the years passed, the face took on new determination and self-assurance. It was the face of a loner. The war aged the face. It made it more sad, more tender, more tired, more spiritual. It gave him the face of an old man. On the trip to Gettysburg Lincoln was fifty-four years old.

On the first leg of the journey Lincoln sat in the partitioned-off portion of the rear car and thumbed through a day-old copy of the *New York Herald* offered him by Lieutenant Henry Cochrane, who was in charge of the Marine band on board. Lincoln thanked the lieutenant. "I like to see what they say about us," he remarked.

New York's morning newspapers arrived in Washington twelve hours late and so made good evening reading for capital-dwellers who had already been marauded by newsboys hawking Washington's morning papers, the *Chronicle* and the *Intelligencer*, followed by Baltimore's dailies — the *Sun*, the *Clipper*, and the *American*. About nine o'clock in the morning, Philadelphia's *Inquirer* and *Press* would arrive by train.

At 2:00 P.M. the first editions of the *Washington Star* and the *Washington Republican* hit the streets. And it was not until dark that a train arrived bearing New York's *Herald*, *Times*, *Tribune*, and *World*. Of these four, the *Herald*, which Lincoln was scanning this morning, was considered the most sensational, the greatest distorter of the facts. The front page of this particular edition seemed mild, though, consisting mainly of a four-column map of the Texas expedition.

It was a simple, slow world that Lincoln read about on the way to Gettysburg. The progress of the war usually dominated most U.S. newspapers these days, but Lincoln would only skim the war stories, saying he knew all about what was happening on the battlefields anyway. Today, though, the Commander in Chief was amused by the wild guesses the paper made about future troop movements. At one point he laughed out loud — much to the pleasure of Lieutenant Cochrane, who delighted in seeing the President's face light up. News of the rest of the world was late and fragmentary, but on normal days Lincoln was usually curious enough to see what was being said in the press to send a secretary for a paper, or even to stroll from the White House grounds in the early morning and find a newsboy down the street himself. Actually, the President usually only "skirmished" (as he put it) through newspapers, picking up a catchword here, another there, to keep close to the pulse of the country.

This week the big news came from Poland, where a revolution against Russian occupation was taking place. Small, angry bands of Polish guerrillas were being formed, and an attempt had been made on the life of a Russian general; a bomb had been lobbed at him as he rode down the streets of Warsaw.

Afghanistan was undergoing one of its usual sieges; a volcano was erupting off the coast of Sicily; smallpox was flourishing in Panama; and France was making military moves in both Mexico and Siam. Elsewhere, an astronomer had spotted a new comet in the heavens; the queen of

England had taken a ride through the grounds of Windsor Castle accompanied by the crown princess of Russia; Brazil and its coffee industry were thriving under the reign of Pedro II; New Zealand was inaugurating its very first railroad; in Central Africa a Dr. Baskie was tracking what he was sure was a unicorn; and Japan's new and highly secret silk moth had just been smuggled into France (under Japanese law, the crime called for the death penalty).

Lincoln was interested in the activities on the high seas. Steam navigation had been developing at a rapid pace and great shipping companies like Cunard and White Star had been put together; the comings and goings and occasional wreckings of their ships filled up a lot of newspaper space. During this particular week, the *Invincible* had sailed from San Francisco bound for Boston with a cargo that included 13,500 hides, 12,000 hams, 560 cases of oil, 13,500 sacks of ore, 471 bales of wool, and 100 boxes of California produce. Storms and ships lost at sea always made good reading. This week the Canadian steamer *Frank Stewart* had broken in two; the *Mesopotamia* had been driven ashore; the *Venturia* had been totally wrecked, with loss of bottom and bilge; and the steamer *Watch Witch* had foundered in a gale, all hands lost.

Closer to home, Lincoln could read about the latest murders, robberies, poisonings, and acts of arson, as well as some news that concerned him more personally: a delegation of Cherokee Indians had just arrived in Washington to see him; Governor Richard Yates of his home state of Illinois had attended the opening of the Atlantic & Great Western Railroad in Cleveland; the Honorable J. R. Giddings, U.S. consul general in Montreal and a violent antislavery advocate, had been arrested for alleged kidnapping; all Southern women in cities occupied by the Yankees had decided to protest against Lincoln by removing the hoops from their skirts.

A few stories were on the lighter side. To win a ninety-dollar bet, one J. J. Gray walked on all fours for one mile without ever straightening up. A device to stop snoring had been invented: it consisted simply of a tube leading from the snorer's mouth to his ear. And then there was the untimely death at sixteen of "The Calculating Boy" in Scotland who could instantaneously tell a person how many seconds he or she had lived, only requiring the birth date, and never failing to make allowance for leap years.

What a bounteous, unspoiled country was reported on! No wonder Lincoln exulted so in his beloved democracy and what that form of government could bring to human life. This particular week the President could read of 140,586 new immigrants in just New York City alone since the beginning of the year; of the nation's 38,183 houses of worship; of new patents galore, including one for the very first dishwashing machine; of workers uniting everywhere to protect their rights; of seven million bushels of wheat received in Chicago over the past two months; of a growing petroleum business and great foreign imports of every nature; of a booming fur trade with 3,500 bison, 28,000 mink, and 250,000 muskrat killed so far in 1863.

The newspapers also reported on the preparations going on at Gettysburg.

As the train clickety-clacked along on its seventy-minute run to Baltimore, Lincoln put down his paper and contemplated the passing scenery. To Lieutenant Cochrane, in the next seat, he remarked on the change he noticed in the kind of ship that sailed the Chesapeake today. Lincoln had first seen the waters and harbors of the great bay when starting out as a thirty-eight-year-old congressman in 1847, and he still remembered the big square-riggers. Now all the craft he spotted looked small.

Except for the musicians, who had already struck up some tunes in the front car, most of the passengers seemed tentative in their actions — as if they couldn't quite decide whether it was proper to be jovial or solemn. Most just sat and swayed with the train, their hands folded across their laps; others stood in the aisles, held on to the backs of the seats, watched the countryside go by. A few talked quietly.

There was plenty to talk about. Eighteen sixty-three had been a different kind of year for Lincoln so far, one filled with a turn for the better on the battlefield but less and less support from his own political party. The President seemed more stooped now, more fragile, his face lined. The year 1861, his first in office, had been a time of transition and, of course, had marked the start of the war. Back then he seemed uncertain of himself, unwilling to take complete command. His high hopes for keeping the Union together without bloodshed had been shattered by the April capture of Fort Sumter, then the defeat at Harpers Ferry, and finally, as skirmishes between North and South became real battles, the July disaster on the banks of a sluggish little stream a mere twenty-five miles from the capital: Bull Run. After eighty-some years, was the democratic experiment in the new world of promise coming apart? As far back as 1838, still in his twenties, Lincoln had anticipated how it would happen if it ever did:

"At what point then is the approach of danger to be expected? I answer, if it ever reach us, it must spring up amongst us. It cannot come from abroad. If destruction be our lot, we must ourselves be its author and finisher. As a nation of freemen, we must live through all time, or die by suicide."

Now, a quarter of a century later, to prevent that suicide, to save that Union, became Lincoln's obsession. The democracy that had been fixed upon by the Founding Fathers was, in Lincoln's opinion, the best form of government anyone had ever conceived. The problem of its preservation, in his opinion, was of a higher importance than any of the individual problems posed by members of its sectors. Those lesser problems would eventually be worked out if the Union remained intact.

In the beginning Lincoln's war strategy seemed simple; he articulated it to a friend soon after Bull Run.

I intend to make and keep the blockade as effective as I can; that is very difficult to do, and it gives me a great deal of trouble, as the line of coast is long; but I attach great importance to that measure, and I mean to do the best I can about it; then I want to move a column of the army into East Tennessee to liberate the Union sentiment there; I want to press them here in Virginia, and keep them away from Washington; I want to hem in those who are fighting us, and make a feint against Richmond, and drive them away from Manassas; I hope ultimately they will get tired of it, and arouse and say to their leaders and to their politicians, "This thing has got to stop!" That is our only chance. It is plain to me that it's no use of trying to subdue those people if they remain united and bound they won't be subdued.

In theorizing about the war, Lincoln was already showing what a personal crusade he regarded it and that he, as Commander in Chief, would lead that crusade — but it would be a humane one, relying on wearing the enemy down rather than savaging it.

Eighteen sixty-two had been dark and forbidding: it began with the death of eleven-year-old Willie. Union forces were making progress striking at Southern defenses across the three great rivers that cut into the Confederacy — the Tennessee, the Cumberland, and the Mississippi. Closer to home, Stonewall Jackson's sixteen thousand graycoats were raiding up and down the Shenandoah Valley from March till June, and Robert E. Lee was proving himself an adroit and imaginative commander by outmaneuvering the Union forces on the Yorktown Peninsula, southwest of Richmond, the Confederacy's capital. Unknown names suddenly became engraved in the nation's history. The names of towns and cities came to mean something different overnight. Antietam, the bloodiest day in America's history, was followed in December by Fredericksburg, with the disastrous Union attempt to take Marye's Heights under blistering, impossible Confederate fire.

Through it all Lincoln was searching for a military leader. The war had begun under the direction of the aging, corpulent, gout-ridden Winfield Scott, remnant of the Mexican War, who couldn't mount a horse anymore and wheezed through his ineffectual days. All hopes that General Irvin McDowell, "the Eater," would push to victory vanished with Bull Run. McClellan — "Little Mac" — proved himself an able builder of fortifications and army discipline but he would not fight. Ambrose Everett Burnside, despite his ornate name, was just plain incompetent, and "Fighting Joe" Hooker wasn't much better. Lincoln watched the parade of Southern generals grow longer and more distinguished with each ensuing battle: Robert E. Lee, P. G. T. Beauregard, Stonewall Jackson, Jeb Stuart, James Longstreet — the names came at him day and night.

Eighteen sixty-three had begun on a high note with the issuing of the Emancipation Proclamation. Before it the war had been slow and aimless — the South eager to fight, the North reluctant. Now the war had suddenly turned into a fierce crusade. To those closest to him the prairie man was emerging as a President of commanding intellect, a strategist, a remarkable leader. But on the floor of the House, his own party had turned against him, denouncing him for inefficiency, shortsightedness, stupidity. There were even rumors of an impeachment movement. And to add to Lincoln's grief, his wife, with her Southern background, was being called a spy in the White House. A secret Senate committee meeting was called to debate these charges.

"We had just been called to order by the Chairman," a member of the committee recalled, "when the officer stationed at the committee room door came in with a half-frightened expression on his face. Before he had opportunity to make explanation, we understood the reason for his excitement, and were ourselves almost overwhelmed with astonishment. For at the foot of the Committee table, standing solitary, his hat in his hand, his form towering, Abraham Lincoln stood. . . . No one spoke," the senator explained, "for no one knew what to say. The President had not been asked to come before the Committee, nor was it suspected that

OPPOSITE: *It was a sad face, yet strong and noble. The left eye wandered. Whiskers made him look older. (Alexander Gardner took this portrait three days before the trip to Pennsylvania.)*

he had information that we were to investigate reports which, if true, fastened treason upon his family in the White House."

Slowly, carefully, the President made his statement. "I, Abraham Lincoln, President of the United States, appear of my own volition before this Committee of the Senate to say that I, of my own knowledge, know that it is untrue that any of my family hold treasonable communication with the enemy."

Those who remembered Lincoln that day remembered a man bowed with almost unbelievable pain and sadness.

SIX

EVEN though the B&O Railroad had issued special tickets to those authorized to travel on Lincoln's train to Gettysburg, no one kept an official roster of who was on board. The most distinguished riders besides the President himself were the three cabinet members Lincoln had been able to persuade to come along: Seward, Blair, and Usher. The first two were among the original seven men Lincoln had chosen to head his administration; Usher was a replacement.

What a curious cabinet Lincoln had appointed. Seward at State, Chase at the Treasury, Bates in Justice, Blair as postmaster general, Welles overseeing the navy, and Smith at the Interior Department — not a single Illinois friend among them. Most, in fact, were his rivals. It was a cabinet largely decided upon the day following Lincoln's nomination, after the tense evening he had spent in Springfield's telegraph office getting word of the convention results from Chicago. "I was there without leaving," Lincoln later recalled, "after the returns began to come in until we had enough to satisfy us as to how the election had gone. I went home, but not to get much sleep, for I felt then, as I never had before, the responsibility that was upon me. I began to feel at once that I needed support — others to share with me the burden. This was on Wednesday morning, and, before the sun went down, I had made up my Cabinet. It was almost the same that I finally appointed."

The least likely of all the candidates for the Republican nomination in 1860, Lincoln actually had won out over four of the original seven men he chose to help run his government — the great senators William Henry Seward of New York and Salmon P. Chase of Ohio, as well as the powerful old war-horse Edward Bates of Missouri and the tricky, conniving Simon Cameron of Pennsylvania. Among the other cabinet secretaries, Montgomery Blair represented not only one of the strongest political families in the country but also the crucial border states. Gideon Welles was a Connecticut newspaper editor who would serve as New England's advocate; he had correctly described Lincoln's character and his potential for greatness before the candidate from Illinois became a national figure. And the remaining cabinet appointee, Indiana's Caleb Blood Smith, had made a deal with Lincoln's people at the convention, even though the man they represented had sent word from Springfield: "I authorize no bargains and will be bound by none." After much soul-searching, Lincoln eventually was bound not only by the bargain struck for Indiana's votes but also by a convention deal with the untrustworthy Cameron, who controlled the Pennsylvania delegation.

This cabinet, though a curious assortment, was a brilliant gathering-together by Lincoln. It not only represented all the political factions that wanted the Union to stand, but also was a very real and surprising attempt at conciliation. The President-elect had put aside his personal preferences, men that he would feel comfortable with, and had concocted instead a group that would represent all the dissident elements that backed the preservation of the Union. Lincoln was consciously and carefully planning for the unspeakable battle ahead.

By now, three years later, Caleb Smith had resigned as secretary of the interior because of bad health and had been replaced by John Palmer Usher, a Terre Haute lawyer who had been born in New York but had spent most of his life in Indiana and become its attorney general. Al-

Secretary of the Interior John Palmer Usher was one of three cabinet members to accompany Lincoln on the special train to Gettysburg. (The print reproduced here, along with many others in this book, was made directly from Mathew Brady's original negative.)

though Noah Brooks once called the pink-skinned, blue-eyed Usher "fair, fat, fifty and florid, well-fed, unctuous," he made a good traveling companion for the President. Usher, who had once ridden the Eighth Circuit with Lincoln, was pleasant and easygoing, as well as knowledgeable in his department. He had charge of the country's mines, the census, and

Also off to Gettysburg with the President was Postmaster General Montgomery Blair, shown here using one of Brady's prop books as an armrest.

all the problems of the Indian tribes in the United States; he also had pensions to give out and the patent office to run, as well as bearing responsibility for education, public buildings, and the care of the surfaces of the streets of Washington.

Usher was objective and he did not hesitate to express himself on the subjects of Lincoln and the personalities around the President in his daily work. He thought Secretary of the Treasury Chase had ability but was selfish and conceited and had purposely had his portrait by Henry Ulke, a very handsome one, put on the one-dollar bill so it would get the greatest circulation. He thought Chase would be given pleasure by any mistake Lincoln might make, whereas Secretary Seward was very kind and very anxious that the President not make "a spectacle of himself," always instructing him how to stand, what to say, and generally how to conduct himself properly. If anything, Usher thought Lincoln was too good, too nice. He was amazed at how Lincoln could refuse people's requests and still have them leave in good humor; no one ever felt inclined to be rude to Lincoln — it was unthinkable. Lincoln never pretended to be wiser than anyone else, but, thought Usher, he was so reasonable and fair that he stood out among and above others. He never blamed anyone for drinking or swearing, but somehow people just didn't drink or swear when he was with them. "When he appeared," said Usher, "everyone seemed to be happy."

Also on the train to Gettysburg this day was Postmaster General Montgomery Blair — Monty, a few of his close friends called him, but most people, including his wife, addressed him as "the Judge." Six feet tall, thin, with blue eyes, a high forehead, and an erect military bearing, the fifty-year-old Blair was the best educated in Lincoln's cabinet, a fine lawyer and financial expert — and the son of Francis P. Blair, who had been Andrew Jackson's ghostwriter and closest confidant, and more than any other man, father of the Republican party when it was created in 1856. The wealthy Jacksonian had gone a long way toward assuring a position for his son by astutely traveling to Springfield in the late 1850s and exchanging very similar political views with Lincoln. Later, after being nominated for President, Lincoln turned to the Blairs for help with a function he knew was of utmost importance in the preservation of the Union: keeping the border states from secession. Since the Blair influence was profound in the key states of Missouri and Maryland, giving young Blair his new job was a masterful appointment, even though Lincoln's advisers didn't think so and kept telling the President-elect that he wasn't really appointing Monty — that the real source of the power he wanted sat seven miles south of Washington in a mansion at Silver Spring, the Blair country estate. It was the senior Blair, also, to whom Lincoln turned — unfortunately for the Union, to no avail — when Robert E. Lee was vacillating over which side to fight on.

By far the most important of Lincoln's guests on the trip was his secretary of state, William H. Seward. Leader of the antislavery faction, Seward had been the most disappointed of the candidates to join Lincoln's cabinet, for he had been the most convinced that he himself should and would win the nomination. But this afternoon, joining his commander on the lurching train, whatever bitterness the eminent redhead who had dared to run for governor of New York at thirty-three felt toward "the prairie lawyer" — he had called Lincoln that before coming to respect him — had long ago disappeared. Only five feet, four inches tall, gangling in build, with a beak for a nose, thick lips that trembled, a weak chin that fell away sharply, huge ears, a tiny neck, and long, thin arms, Seward kept a yellow silk handkerchief constantly at hand to stifle his snuff-provoked sneezes, and his old-fashioned clothes reeked of his chain-smoked cigars. Affable, a nonstop talker and unrestrained storyteller, a lover of good food, wine, and gossip, a student of the classics and the theater, and a devoted husband to an invalid wife, the secretary of state had become Lincoln's closest adviser.

At first people thought Seward was really running the country as

Lincoln's most eminent guest on the trip was his kind and brilliant secretary of state, close adviser William H. Seward.

the bumpkin Lincoln told his funny stories and pretended to be President. Actually Lincoln listened to Seward — and then did exactly what he himself felt was right, whether it followed the advice or not. Often frustrated with his leader but never really annoyed, Seward moved from his original state of shock to a real affection for Lincoln and a respect and admiration for his remarkable mind. The feeling was mutual; it was Seward whom Lincoln had turned to for advice on the wording of the Emancipation Proclamation — and now, on this very night ahead, Lincoln would turn to Seward again for advice: on the most compelling set of words he would ever put together.

SEVEN

MANY of the details of Lincoln's train trip to Gettysburg will remain forever untold. No one recorded just when the President began to perk up and feel himself again. Neither Nicolay nor Hay took down the luncheon menu. No reporter or diarist described all the sights that whizzed by out the little square windows on both sides of the President's car. And no one told what songs were sung by the reporters and played by the Marine musicians and members of the other band on board; or whether or not Lieutenant Fred Jackson of the Invalid Corps told how a Rebel surgeon had amputated his left arm after he had been hit by canister early in the war; or how Secretary of War Edwin Stanton's son occupied himself during the trip; or just where Edward Everett's daughter and her husband sat; or whether the Senate chaplain, T. H. Stockton, said grace before lunch; or whether Henri Mercier, the French minister, or Joseph

Bertinatti, the Italian minister, joined Lincoln in a storytelling session after lunch. We do know, though, that General Fry, the President's special escort, did not remember Lincoln working on the address he was to deliver the next day. "I have no recollection of seeing him writing or even reading his speech during the journey," said Fry. Long afterward, however, a few other passengers would disagree with the general.

The French minister to the United States, Henri Mercier, was one of Lincoln's special guests on the trip to Gettysburg. Like many foreign dignitaries, he had posed at Brady's.

We do know, also, that as the train approached Baltimore, Seward grew more and more uneasy. That city had ominous memories for Lincoln, Seward knew; on the trip east from Springfield almost three years ago, a plot to assassinate the President-elect had been hatched in Baltimore — or so Allan Pinkerton's security men had announced — and Lincoln had been sneaked secretly through the city in the dead of night to ride out of town incognito.

But today no one really thought that there would be a repeat performance. At exactly 1:10 P.M. the train slowed at the B&O's Bolton station. After the locomotive had come to its hissing halt, Lincoln stepped out onto the rear platform of his coach to greet the enthusiastic gathering of railroad officials and two hundred other admirers who cheered him noisily. Two babies were thrust up at the President by excited mothers and Lincoln obediently kissed each one. With the passengers still inside, the railroad cars were now unhitched, and tandem teams of horses slowly dragged them one by one, on tracks usually used only for freight cars, to the Calvert Street station of the Northern Central. During re-assembly a windowless baggage car, to be used as a makeshift dining car for the day, was inserted between the third car and the President's. A Baltimore lad, Andrew B. Staley, had the privilege of being the train's news- and candy-boy for this next stage of the run.

At 2:00 P.M., just before departure, General James Findlay Schenck, wounded veteran of Bull Run, boarded the train along with his staff. General William Morris, in command of the defenses of Baltimore, sent his regrets to the President: he was suffering from boils. This prompted Lincoln to tell a story to his postmaster general. "Blair, did you ever know that fright has sometimes proved a sure cure for boils?" Lincoln asked with a quizzical expression.

"No, Mr. President. How is that?" Blair replied.

Lincoln proceeded to tell about a certain colonel out on reconnaissance who was troubled "with a big boil where it made horseback riding decidedly uncomfortable." The colonel had dismounted to relieve himself of the pain when suddenly the rebels attacked. Into the saddle the colonel sprang and made capital time over fences and ditches until he was safe behind his own lines. The colonel swore that when he dismounted this time the boil was gone, and he commented, "The secession has rendered to loyalty one valuable service at any rate."

Now John Eckert, the new conductor, signaled the engineer, and shortly after 2:00 P.M. the reassembled train with its added car and new engine chugged northward out of Baltimore toward Pennsylvania.

The tall hat that Lincoln was wearing looked as if a calf had licked it — he never sponged it with vinegar or stale beer as *Miss Leslie's Lady's House-Book* directed. Inside, stuck into an inner band, there were some papers: maybe his Riggs Bank book, showing the President's latest monthly salary deposit of $2,083.33; surely a few letters, notes he had

Lincoln's stovepipe hat. Tucked inside he kept important papers — including, in November of 1863, a draft of his Gettysburg speech.

jotted on subjects he wanted to remember; and — most important of all — the folded paper on which he had been preparing the short address he would make the following day.

The high hat that acted as Lincoln's briefcase was symbolic of how much the outer man had changed since the presidency had been won. Early Illinois friends remembered him in flax trousers (inches too short for his long, gangly legs and held up by a single suspender), a calico shirt, brogans, and blue yarn socks — all topped off by a straw hat, its rim turned up in the back. Dressing up for Lincoln in those days meant a blue-jean coat — claw-hammer style — homespun linen trousers, and stogie boots. Even later, after he had married and was a highly respected lawyer and politician, Lincoln was a man of shirt sleeves, slippers, an old wrapper, patched trousers, rough shoes, and faded brown hat with its nap worn off. Out on the circuit he carried an old green umbrella, a piece of twine wrapped round it to keep it from flying open; and in his carpet-

Lincoln's hatbox atop a stool

bag were a jumble of papers, long-sleeved cotton undershirts, under-shorts, some stockings, a bone-handled toothbrush, and a long, coarse, yellow flannel nightshirt that reached halfway between his knees and his feet.

Mrs. Lincoln could do little about her casually dressed husband, although she spoke to him sharply and often about his appearance. It wasn't until 1860, however, that Lincoln, still a political unknown on the national scene, truly embarrassed himself by the way he looked: when he came into New York to speak before an audience of the city's most elegant in the stately Cooper Union and brought only a rumpled, poorly fitting new suit. And so, late in the same year, after the electorate had made its surprising selection, a welcome present arrived in Springfield all the way from Brooklyn. It was from a hatter. Lincoln put the formal high hat on, inspected himself, looked at Mrs. Lincoln, back at the re-flection, back again at her, and finally said, "Well, Wife, there is one thing likely to come out of this scrape, anyhow. We are going to have some new clothes."

At first he didn't really know how to wear those new clothes, and the crop of young whiskers he was growing didn't help his appearance at his inauguration. On that occasion he wore a black dress coat, a satin vest, black dress pants, and a glossy high hat; in his hand was a large ebony cane with a gold head. Once on the platform, the uncomfortable Lincoln became confused as to what to do with his hat and cane. Who but his lifelong arch-rival, the Springfield man who had vied with him for Mary Todd's hand, the politician he had debated against so many times, the Democratic candidate for President he had so recently defeated — who but Stephen A. Douglas stepped forward, kindly took the hat, and held it while in a distinct, ringing voice Lincoln addressed his entire country for the very first time.

During the run from Baltimore to Hanover Junction, Lincoln and his personal guests took lunch. In the converted baggage car the President sat at the head of a long makeshift table and ate sparingly while telling amusing stories. With Lincoln back in his car at the next stop along the way, a little lisping girl was raised up to an open window so she could hand the President a bunch of rosebuds. She got a kiss in return as Lincoln told her, "You're a sweet little rosebud yourself."

At one point the train slowed enough for a man to swing himself up onto the steps and come aboard. This new passenger sought out the President and, without trouble from those charged with security, engaged him in conversation. The intruder wanted to tell Lincoln that his son had been killed at Gettysburg fighting on Little Round Top. "A visit to that spot, I fear, will open your wounds afresh," the President commiserated. "But oh, dear sir, if we had reached the end of such sacrifices, and had nothing left for us to do but place garlands on the grass of those already fallen, we could give thanks even amidst our tears; but when I think of the sacrifices of life yet to be offered and the hearts and homes yet to be made desolate before this dreadful war is over, I feel at times like hiding in deep darkness."

In the front section of Lincoln's car a group of men were telling stories. Lincoln joined them, told some rollicking good ones, then, after almost an hour, excused himself. "Gentlemen," he said, "this is all very pleasant, but the people will expect me to say something to them tomorrow, and I must give the matter some thought."

Hanover Junction, some fifty miles north of Baltimore, wasn't much of a town. An early directory listed eight residents — all men: two who ran a general store, one hotel proprietor, an ice-cream manufacturer, a wagon maker, a blacksmith, a grain dealer, and a butcher. It was here at Hanover Junction that the President's train was scheduled to join up with the Governors' Special, a train that had originated in Harrisburg and had aboard not only Andrew Curtin of Pennsylvania but a host of other governors, dignitaries, and generals, as well as Colonel Robert Anderson, the hero who had been in charge of Fort Sumter at the time of her fall.

But where was the Governors' Special? This train, especially concocted by Governor Curtin for the occasion, turned out to be the last act in a comic-book opera. A train from Cincinnati that was to meet the Governors' Special was delayed nine hours at Coshocton, Ohio, by a freight train crack-up that created impassable wreckage. A train from Wheeling bringing West Virginia's delegation arrived at Harrisburg by mistake in the middle of the night. The Governors' Special was scheduled to leave the Pennsylvania capital at 1:00 P.M. Tuesday but did not finally get off until 3:30 P.M. When its engine broke away from its tender fifteen miles out, tearing the water pipes of the tank in two, another engine had to be sent for. Expecting a good dinner at York, the passengers had to make do with stale gingerbread and persimmons on the station platform at Goldsboro. Night fell and not only was there no heat aboard, the lights didn't work either. The Governors' Special missed its hookup with Lincoln's train by six hours and finally limped into Gettysburg late that night.

At Hanover Junction, Lincoln's train switched over to the Hanover Branch Railroad and then, with a new engine, made the 12.2-mile run to the town of Hanover. Hanover's population of under two hundred was out in force to watch Lincoln's train go through. They were to get a special treat: an actual look at the President and a short speech from him as well, for a train going east forced Lincoln's train to halt for eight minutes.

Representing the little Hanover crowd, the Reverend M. J. Alleman climbed aboard Lincoln's car, approached the President, and said, "Father Abraham, your children want to see you." It was not a good way to begin; Lincoln was not fond of being addressed as "Abe" or "Abraham" — and especially not as "Father Abraham." He even disliked "Mr. Lincoln" and "Mr. President," preferring just plain "Lincoln." If a title was necessary, what about "attorney for the people"? he asked. Nevertheless, he now followed the preacher out onto the rear platform and was greeted by loud applause. The *Philadelphia Inquirer* reported that Lincoln then "delivered one of the brief, quaint speeches for which he is celebrated. Said he: 'Well, you have seen me. . . . you had the rebels here last summer. . . . did you fight them any?' The people looked at each other with a half-amused, half-puzzled expression," the *Inquirer* report continued, "while the long, lean form of the President leaned from the car as he waited their reply. The ladies came forward, bringing bouquets and presented them to the President, while a beautiful flag, the work of the women in the neighborhood, was placed in the rear of the car. The whistle screamed . . . and the car rattled up the Gettysburg Road."

That kind of impromptu speech was so different from the times Lincoln was prepared and really had something to say. Especially if that something had passion behind it. Bidding his beloved Springfield good-bye almost three years before was a good example. In the carriage to the station, his newly appointed young secretary John Nicolay helped with the few words he would say to his fellow townspeople from the rear platform of the train just before departure. They were words filled with the emotion of leaving — as it turned out, for good — the place that was his home and the only friends he was really close to. Years of public speaking, much of it before these very people, had prepared Lincoln for this moment. He could have gone on at length about his career and his feelings for Springfield and the mission that lay ahead. Instead his words were few, the ideas infused with the emotion not only of the moment but of the times. Lincoln was not merely leaving his house, his dog, his practice, the grave of his son: he was saying good-bye to a successful, comfortable life and embarking on an uncertain voyage.

TOP: *The only house Lincoln ever owned. In 1844 he bought it for $1,500 from the minister who had performed his marriage ceremony. (The picture was taken in 1860 by John Adams Whipple, a Boston newsman who was visiting Springfield.)*

BOTTOM: *In this enlarged detail from the same photograph, Lincoln is seen standing behind the fence with his son Willie. Tad, the youngest Lincoln, is barely visible, peeking out from behind the fence post.*

The Lincoln house as it looked from behind

"My friends," he began on that cold, rainy February morning, "no one, not in my situation, can appreciate my feeling of sadness at this parting. To this place, and the kindness of these people, I owe every thing. Here I have lived a quarter of a century, and have passed from a young to an old man. Here my children have been born, and one is buried. I now leave, not knowing when or whether ever I may return, with a task before me greater than that which rested upon Washington."

The crowd of a thousand friends and acquaintances, huddled beneath umbrellas to shield them from the drizzle, pressed closer to hear the few remaining words of the tall, thin man they had watched for years wandering their streets lost in thought, playing stickball with children, separating right from wrong by fireside; the man who endlessly told stories, who was seen so many times leaving his second-story office to amble home and milk his cow; their very special, rather strange fellow citizen — the man of their town in whom they took the most pride.

Referring again to George Washington, Lincoln continued: "Without the assistance of that Divine Being, who ever attended him, I cannot succeed. With that assistance I cannot fail. Trusting in Him, who can go with me, and remain with you and be everywhere for good, let us confidently hope that all will yet be well. To His care commending you, as I hope in your prayers you will commend me, I bid you an affectionate farewell."

OPPOSITE: *The Springfield train station from which President-elect Lincoln departed for Washington in early 1861. It was here that he met one last time with his Illinois friends and neighbors, shaking their hands and kissing some of the well-wishers good-bye inside the little brick building. Just before leaving, he made his farewell address to the people of his town from the rear platform of a special train that had been assembled to start him on his journey east.*

On the final approach to Gettysburg, darkness dimmed the ravaged countryside.

EIGHT

IT was dusk in the town of Gettysburg and people were all over the tracks, crowding around the little depot on Carlisle Street in anticipation of the President's arrival. Decorated with the American colors and with intertwined wreaths of jessamine and evergreen that encircled the headlight reflector, the locomotive was heaving up and down the last few hills. On board, Wayne Mac-Veagh, the chairman of the Pennsylvania Republican Central Committee, had Lincoln's ear and was talking — too loudly — about Missouri affairs. Almost reckless talk it was. Finally MacVeagh realized he was out of line and quieted down, even though it was a rare opportunity for a politician like him to collar the President. Through the windows of the train the passengers could only dimly see the countryside on the final approach. It looked so peaceful: the orchards and fields, the symmetrical white fences and running stone walls, finally the shapes of houses and the sprinkling of lights.

The Scotch-Irish village was less than a hundred years old; it had been founded by James Getty in 1780, and when the countryside around it had been measured off and officially stamped with the name of Adams County in 1800, Gettysburg became its natural center. By the 1860s the town's population had grown to 2,300. Carriage making and education had sprung up as Gettysburg's two main industries. Ten small plants built carriages of all shapes and sizes, and in or nearby the town were the Pennsylvania College of Gettysburg (known as Gettysburg College), the Lutheran Theological Seminary, and a school for girls run by Miss Carrie Shead.

Radiating from the town like carriage spokes were eleven different roads. Two led to cities — Baltimore and Harrisburg; four to other towns — York, Carlisle, Hanover, and Hagerstown; the rest to hamlets — Hunterstown, Taneyville, Emmitsburg, Chambersburg, and Mummasburg.

A view of the Pennsylvania College of Gettysburg, which was used as a hospital during and after the battle

The train halted, hissing its brake steam, and there was the President, his black suit and high hat and extraspecial height distinguishing him from the others on the platform. A cheer from the crowd. A pleasant greeting to this central guest, who showed some weariness in his familiar smile. Along with an unpleasant greeting: the sight of piled coffins on the station platform. Some families did not want their boys buried so far away and were taking them back home instead.

Through the crowd came old friend Lamon and along with him a man three years Lamon's junior. The President had heard a good deal about this David Wills. And Mr. Everett was there too, to greet his daughter and his son-in-law and to shake Lincoln's hand, and here amidst all the to-do were others whom the President knew and recognized, among them General Darius Couch. Now they were all trying to extricate the President from the gentle, admiring mob. Up through a gauntlet of soldiers Lincoln went, people's hands reaching over to touch him on the way, three hundred paces or thereabouts to the imposing Wills house on "the Diamond," the town square.

The President climbed the steep front stairs to the second floor of the elegant house and was shown to a handsome room with canopied four-poster that was to be his for the night. Strains of a serenade in the President's honor lifted from songsters outside.

For days people had been piling into the little town, coming by train and by carriage and by horseback and on foot. Now Gettysburg was jam-packed. Bonfires shot sprays of sparks into the night sky, torches lit the streets, people edged and pushed and shoved their ways about, looking for a place to buy a decent dinner, searching for a spot to sleep. Not an empty bed was to be had for miles around; they had all been spoken for days earlier, along with the pew benches in the churches, even the tavern floors, the hotel lobbies, and the boardinghouse parlors. People slapped each other on the back, sang, and made speeches. Pickpockets worked the crowd and whiskey flowed freely.

Colonel Lamon, in charge of tomorrow's ceremony, was holding a final meeting of his marshals in the local courthouse, which had been specially warmed for the occasion. Over and over again Lamon repeated the details of what was expected of his seventy-two men and explained where they would pick up their horses and special badges the next morning. When he was finally done, someone proposed that a donation be made by the assembled men to help the Union prisoners in Richmond's notorious Libby Prison. A hat was passed and $160 was collected, including $10 pledged by Secretary of State Seward, who had wandered into the meeting. "Put that down for Marshall Seward, an individual," he called out.

Irreverent, fun-loving John Hay painted the scene of that night in his diary. As soon as the train arrived

our party broke like a drop of quicksilver split. MacVeagh, young Stanton and I foraged around for a while, . . . walked out to the College, got a chafing dish of oysters, then some supper, and, finally, loafing around to the Court House where Lamon was holding a meeting of marshalls, we found [newspaperman John] Forney, and went around to his place . . . and drank a little wiskey [*sic*] with him. . . . We went out after a while following the music to hear the serenades. . . . We went back to Forney's room, having picked up Nicolay, and drank more whiskey. Nicolay sang his little song of the "Three Thieves," and we then sang "John Brown."

While Nicolay was a frail, serious man who tired easily and was often in poor health, Hay was vigorous and witty, a juggler of words. He had been class poet at Brown University and had been a lively addition to the Lincoln entourage ever since Lincoln had accepted the need for an assistant secretary to aid Nicolay ("Well, let Hay come," the President-elect had said reluctantly back in Springfield).

On this gay and bibulous night in Gettysburg, Hay's mind certainly wasn't on business. Several times he was stopped on the streets by reporters and asked for a copy of what the President planned to say tomorrow. With a shrug he had to turn each request down. He probably wasn't even wondering what "the Tycoon" — one of his and Nicolay's private names for Lincoln (another was "the Ancient") — had up his sleeve for the morrow. Hay would have had at least a hint if he had remembered a conversation he'd had with Lincoln two and a half years earlier. The subject was the war and the President was talking casually, as he often did with Hay.

Despite his fragility, presidential secretary John Nicolay accompanied Lincoln on the trip to Gettysburg and joined in the revelry that took place on the night before the ceremonies.

John Hay, the glib, spirited assistant secretary to the President, brought youthful zest to Lincoln's staff.

"For my own part," Lincoln had said, "I consider the central idea pervading this struggle is the necessity that is upon us of proving that popular government is not an absurdity. We must settle this question now, whether, in a free government, the minority have the right to break up the government whenever they choose. If we fail, it will go far to prove the incapability of the people to govern themselves. . . . Taking the government as we found it, we will see if the majority can preserve it."

The theme of the possible fragility of democracy would emerge again, the next day, in quite different words: "Now we are engaged in a great civil war, testing whether that nation, or any nation so conceived and so dedicated, can long endure."

The Willses' dinner table was set for twenty-four this evening, a lavish display of silver and china and linen under ornate candelabra. The sweeping and shining and ironing and polishing had been going on for days, followed by the baking and boiling and roasting — and now all was in ready. The dinner went off smoothly. The dining room was a din of talk, clacking knives and forks, and occasional laughter. Lincoln, Edward Everett wrote in his diary, sat "by the side of several distinguished persons, ladies and gentlemen, Foreigners and Americans, among them the French minister at Washington . . . and the admiral of the French Fleet." Yet the President, to Everett's surprise, was "in gentlemanly appearance, manners and conversation . . . the peer of any man at the table." In Everett's judgment, Lincoln certainly did not fit his common description "as a person of uncouth appearance and manners."

Outside, exuberant musicians from the Fifth New York Artillery band were joined by the members of glee clubs and by other serenaders. It was nine o'clock now, and insistent calls went up from the crowd demanding speeches from the diners inside, especially Everett and Lincoln. Finishing dinner and grouping in the parlor, the celebrities tried

Mrs. David Wills set an elegant table for the President and twenty-one other dinner guests on the night of Lincoln's arrival.

to ignore the fervant entreaties, but the cries for the President increased until finally, with great reluctance, he went to a window. The crowd cheered wildly, then hushed. At first Lincoln only waved and withdrew, but when the calls for him resumed, he appeared a second time and spoke a few words.

"I appear before you, fellow citizens, merely to thank you for this compliment," the President began. It was obvious that he had nothing at all to say. Why didn't he, as his wife so often implored him, merely wave and disappear instead of making a fool of himself?

"The inference," Lincoln continued, "is a very fair one that you would hear me for a little while at least, were I to commence to make a speech. I do not appear before you for the purpose of doing so, and for several substantial reasons. The most substantial of these is that I have no speech to make."

Here the crowd laughed. Lincoln continued, "In my position, it is somewhat important that I should not say any foolish things."

"If you can help it," a voice called from the crowd.

"It very often happens," Lincoln went right on, "that the only way to help it is to say nothing at all."

Here, more laughter. Lincoln quickly closed.

"Believing that is my present condition this evening, I must beg of you to excuse me from addressing you further."

The Willses' dinner guests now began to participate in a general reception, while Everett retired to hold a press conference, during which he entertained reporters with stories about living in Europe and brushing up against the great. Amid the confusion of introductions and hand-shakes in the Willses' parlor a telegram was delivered to Lincoln from Secretary of War Edwin Stanton in Washington. He was relaying the latest dispatch from General Burnside at Knoxville. "The enemy appear to be holding back for some reason. Burnside expresses confidence in his position." That was good news, but even better was the message that followed: "By inquiry Mrs. Lincoln informed me that your son is better this evening."

The serenaders moved on. At the home of Robert G. Harper, next door, they flushed the secretary of state, who made a long, rather pompous speech beginning: "Fellow citizens, I am now sixty years old and upwards; I have been in public life practically forty years of that time, and yet this is the first time that ever any people or community so near the border of Maryland was found willing to listen to my voice; and the reason for that, I said fifty years ago that slavery was opening before this people a graveyard that was to be filled with brothers falling in mutual political combat. . . ."

Now that the serenaders — a small instrumental ensemble, a group of young women singers, a male quartet — had got both the President and the secretary of state to speak, they began making the rounds to the places other notables were staying and urging them out too, to address the crowds. John Forney, the unpredictable newspaper publisher, was one of a number who were persuaded to speak.

Later, into the Wills house crowded several revelers, including John Hay and Wayne MacVeagh, who had come from John Forney's room, where they had helped persuade the inebriated journalist from Washington and Philadelphia to make his speech to the serenaders. As he had on the train, MacVeagh once again cornered Lincoln, and much to the President's amusement, he now described what the notorious Forney, a frequent visitor at the White House, had said to the performers. Hay recorded it in his diary this way:

Forney said, "if I speak, I will speak my mind." The music sounded in the street, and the fuglers came rushing up, imploring him to come down. He smiled quietly, told them to keep cool, and asked, "are the recorders there?" "I suppose so, of course," shouted up the fugler. "Ascertain!" said the imperturbable Forney. "Hay, we'll take a drink." They shouted and begged him to come down. . . . Somebody commanded prudence. He said sternly, "I am always prudent." . . . Forney stood on the threshold . . . ; the crowd shouted as the door opened. Forney said:

"My friends, these are the first hearty cheers I have heard tonight. You gave no such cheers to your President down the street. Do you know what you owe that great man? You owe your country — you owe your name as American Citizens."

At the finish a friend had said, "That speech must not be written out yet. He will see further about it when he gets sober."

It was well after nine when the President recovered from his mirth over Forney's antics and excused himself, saying, as MacVeagh remembered it, that "he wished to consider further the few words he was expected to say the next day." A young sergeant — H. Paxton Bingham, from the Twenty-first Pennsylvania Cavalry — followed Lincoln up the stairs. It was Bingham's duty to guard the President's door throughout the night; the sentry's long, serious face, accentuated by gruff sideburns, made him look like a good choice.

Now Lincoln sat at a table with his speech before him. He was alone with his Negro valet, William Slade, whom he had brought with him

Sergeant H. Paxton Bingham was assigned to guard Lincoln's bedroom door throughout the night.

from Washington. Slowly the President began to read aloud, a paragraph here, a sentence there. He looked up. "William, now how does that sound?" he kept asking Slade. He didn't really want advice: he wanted to hear the words out loud so as to judge them two ways at once — by eye and by ear.

It was a few minutes before ten when Lincoln sent Slade to ask Mr. Wills if he would please come up. The President did not mention his speech to Wills — or even the fact that he had been working on it; instead, he asked him what exactly was the program for tomorrow and what was he, as President, expected to do. David Wills told him every detail and departed.

The President was still working on his speech at eleven when the Governors' Special, after all its travails, finally arrived in Gettysburg. Soon Andrew Curtin made his entrance and was ushered to the honored guest's room to pay his respects. Shortly thereafter, with Curtin still present, Lincoln sent for David Wills a second time. "When I went to his room, he had the same paper in his hand," Wills recalled. He "asked me if he could see Mr. Seward. I told him Mr. Seward was staying with my neighbor, next door, and I would go and bring him over. He said, 'No, I'll go and see him.'"

Even though only a few steps separated the front doors of the Wills and the Harper houses, the festive crowd was still so thick that both Sergeant Bingham and Governor Curtin had to run interference for the President. Once inside the Harper home, Lincoln conferred alone with Secretary Seward for a full half hour. Outside in the street, the Baltimore Glee Club — twelve voices strong and fresh despite their recent journey aboard the Governors' Special — burst into song. First a brisk "Our Army Is Marching On" was aimed toward the house into which the crowd had seen the President disappear; then a heartfelt rendition of "We Are Coming, Father Abraham" attracted even more revelers, who called out for Lincoln and yipped and clapped their enthusiasm.

The first time Lincoln had sought advice on a speech from Seward was more than two and a half years earlier, before the President's swearing-in. Although Lincoln had written the basis of his inaugural speech in Springfield — it had been set in type and proofed there — he added to it and subtracted from it in Washington. Of all the incoming President's new advisers, Seward was the one who helped him with it most; in fact, his comments caused Lincoln to strike whole paragraphs. Feeling that the close of the speech as Lincoln had it was too threatening ("Shall it be peace, or a sword?"), Seward offered a substitute ending, scrawling out a paragraph he felt was more suitable — "some words of affection," as he put it, "some of calm and cheerful confidence."

"I close," Seward's proposed peroration began, and continued with some critical punctuation not yet inserted.

We are not we must not be aliens or enemies but fellow countrymen and brethren. Although passion has strained our bonds of affection too hardly they must not, I am sure they will not be broken. The mystic chords which proceeding from so many battle fields and so many patriot graves pass through all the hearts and all the hearths in this broad continent of ours will yet again harmonize in their ancient music when breathed upon by the guardian angel of the nation.

Lincoln studied the words of his designated secretary of state and decided to adapt them. He crossed out the ending lines of the speech he had written in Springfield, then took most of Seward's words, reworked them, changed their meaning a bit, inserted a poetic ring in how they were placed, and shortened the whole concluding idea. What resulted are still some of the most moving lines in America's history.

I am loth to close. We are not enemies, but friends. We must not be enemies. Though passion may have strained, it must not break our bonds of affection. The mystic chords of memory, stretching from every battle-field, and patriot grave, to every loving heart and hearthstone, all over this broad land, will yet swell the chorus of the Union, when again touched, as surely they will be, by the better angels of our nature.

Those words had been spoken as war was about to break out; now, after two and a half years of savage fighting, Lincoln again was going over an important speech with his most trusted adviser. How different were these two men, yet how close they had become — and despite their strong rivalry for the job Lincoln had won. "No knife was ever sharp enough to divide us on any question of public policy," declared Seward, "though we frequently arrived at the same conclusion by different processes of thought." And he went even further on another occasion: "Mr. Lincoln is the best man I ever knew."

William Seward carefully read what Lincoln showed him that night in Gettysburg. Small, hollow-chested, sallow-skinned, the secretary of state had a gaze that was indirect and subtle, giving the impression that he was thinking something secret and mysterious. He offered his advice to the President with great courtesy, however, in hushed tones — a change from his usual harsh, guttural voice. Seward was against Lincoln using *proposition* in the opening of the speech (". . . dedicated to the proposition that all men are created equal"); he did not think it was the right word. But Lincoln prevailed. It seems doubtful that the President made even a single change as the result of the half hour he spent with his chief adviser, for surely Seward would have pointed to the specific revision — his personal contribution to the Gettysburg Address — for the rest of his life.

When the Harpers' front door opened again and Lincoln stepped out, the President coaxed old Mr. Harper to come out too, and Lincoln introduced him to the crowd. There was heated applause, and shouts of "Speech! Speech!" were directed at the President.

"I can't speak tonight, gentlemen," Lincoln answered, wary of making the same mistake twice in one evening. "I will see you all tomorrow. Good night." And with this he whispered to Sergeant Bingham, "You clear a way and I will hang on to your coat." The two dived into the crowd and surfaced in a few moments at the Willses' house next door.

There were some final good-nights. David Wills made sure Lincoln needed nothing more. According to Governor Curtin, the President went

Andrew Curtin, governor of Pennsylvania, was scheduled to stay at the Wills house, but when he arrived late there were no beds left.

back to his writing table and seemed "to be copying from the notes on the sheet of foolscap paper." Curtin had expected to spend the night at the Wills house too, but now the embarrassed host informed him that the place was overbooked and all he could offer was half of Mr. Everett's bed.

The very thought of such a thing upset the principal speaker on that night of trepidation before his carefully planned oration. "Parties continued to arrive all the evening," Everett told his diary, "and an immense number of persons filled up the little town. Thirty-eight were lodged at Mr. Wills'. Governor Curtin did not get in till eleven and at first it was proposed to put the Governor into my bed with me. He kindly went out and found a lodging elsewhere."

Everett could sleep in peace, or so he thought. "I did not get to bed till half past eleven; and the fear of having the Executive of Pennsylvania tumble in upon me kept me awake till one. Nervousness about tomorrow no doubt had something to do with my unrest."

The former senator and secretary of state wasn't the only one in the house that night who had trouble sleeping. His daughter, Charlotte Wise, whom he called Charlie, had arrived on the Lincoln train and had attended the splendid Wills dinner. But later "two ladies were put into bed with Charlie," Everett noted in his diary, "the bed broke down, and she betook herself to the floor."

The Wills house finally began to quiet. At midnight, however, the President received another telegram, this one a firsthand message from his wife. "The Doctor has just left," it read. "We hope dear Taddie is slightly better. Will send you a telegram in the morning."

A few seconds after Lincoln read it, Sergeant Bingham got a surprise when the door to the bedroom suddenly swung open and the President stepped into the hall.

"That telegram was from home," Lincoln told the sentry. "My little boy is very sick, but is better."

Soon after midnight the lights in Lincoln's room were extinguished. Still, in the square outside, the singers continued to serenade for another two hours. For some reason Lincoln had been sleeping well lately; after such an exhausting day, the soft strains of "We Are Coming, Father Abraham" did not keep him awake at all this night.

We are coming, Father Abraham, three hundred thousand more
From Mississippi's winding stream and from New England's shore
We leave our plows and workshops, our wives and children dear,
With hearts too full for utterance, with but a silent tear;
We dare not look behind us, but steadfastly before,
We are coming, Father Abra'am, three hundred thousand more.

If you look across the hilltops that meet the northern sky,
Long moving lines of rising dust your vision may descry,
And now the wind, an instant, tears the cloudy veil aside,
And floats aloft our spangled flag in glory and in pride;
And bayonets in the sunlight gleam, and bands brave music pour,
We are coming, Father Abra'am, three hundred thousand more.

NINE

THE 270 or so words that are scratched on the pieces of writing paper beside the sleeping President have not come together by chance, by a lucky stroke of genius. For in a hundred different ways, in a thousand different shapes and guises, Lincoln has been dealing with these concepts his entire adult life: mulling them, talking them, arguing them, writing them down, speaking them from the stump, dreaming them — all the time edging closer and closer to the concentrated form in which he will finally sum up these deepest beliefs with the fire and eloquence of an Old Testament prophet.

How has all this come about? Who is this man and what has been his special road to Gettysburg?

———

In 1637 eighteen-year-old Samuel Lincoln arrives in America from England and settles in Massachusetts.

Samuel marries and has a son Mordecai, who in turn has a son Mordecai, who moves south to New Jersey and then Pennsylvania. And there he has a son John, who lives in Virginia and has a son Abraham, who, filled with dreams of new lands and adventure, strikes off down the perilous Wilderness Road to Kentucky with his friend and kinsman Daniel Boone. And there, in a clearing beside his cabin, in full view of his sons, Abraham is killed by Indians. And one of the young sons he leaves is Thomas, who grows up and does carpentry and marries young Nancy Hanks. And as the first decade of the nineteenth century is coming to an end, on a winter Sunday afternoon in Kentucky, our Abraham Lincoln is born.

"I was born Feb. 12, 1809, in Hardin County, Kentucky," writes Lincoln fifty years later. "My parents were both born in Virginia, of undistinguished families. . . . My father, at the death of his father, was but six years of age; and he grew up literally without education. . . . I was raised to farm work."

"You bet I was tickled to death," remembers Dennis Hanks, an older cousin who grew up with Abe.

Babies wasn't as common as blackberries in the woods o' Kaintucky. Mother come over an' washed him an' put a yaller flannel petticoat on him, an' cooked some dried berries and wild honey fur Nancy, an' slicked things up an' went home. An' that's all the nuss'n either of 'em got. . . . Well, now, he looked just like any other baby, at fust — like red cherry pulp squeezed dry. An' he didn't improve none as he growed older. Abe never was much fur looks. I ricollect how Tom joked about Abe's long legs when he was toddlin' round the cabin. He growed out o' his clothes faster'n Nancy could make 'em.

But he was mighty good comp'ny, solemn as a papoose, but interested in everything. An' he always did have fits o' cuttin' up. I've seen him when he was a little feller, settin' on a stool, starin' at a visitor. All of a sudden he'd bu'st out laughin' fit to kill. If he told us what he was laughin' at, half the time we couldn't see no joke.

OPPOSITE: *Abraham Lincoln's father, Thomas, was as good a storyteller as his son.*

Abe never give Nancy no trouble after he could walk excep' to keep him in clothes. Most o' the time he went bar'foot. Ever wear a wet buckskin glove? Them moccasins wasn't no putection ag'inst the wet. Birch bark with hickory bark soles, strapped on over yarn socks, beat buckskin all holler, fur snow. Abe'n me got purty handy contrivin' things that way. An' Abe was right out in the woods about a soon's he was weaned, fishin' in the creek, settin' traps fur rabbits an' muskrats, goin' on coon-hunts with Tom an' me an' the dogs, follerin' up bees to find bee-trees, an' drappin' corn fur his pappy. Mighty interestin' life fur a boy, but thar was a good many chances he wouldn't live to grow up.

Dennis Hanks, a young cousin of Lincoln's mother's who grew up in the wilderness with the future President, claimed he remembered the day little Abraham was born.

But Abe does live, even though the spindly boy comes close to drowning one day while trying to cross a stream and some years later survives an almost fatal kick in the head by a horse. The Lincolns' log cabin in Kentucky sits on the Old Cumberland Trail, over which lines of slaves are driven south to market. Near a second cabin close by, to which the Lincoln family moves when Abe is four, there are great cliffs of limestone covered with trees, and there are caves, a bubbling spring, thick forests full of game, rich red earth to till and plant.

"I remember that old home very well," Lincoln reminisces.

Our farm was composed of three fields. It lay in the valley, surrounded by high hills and deep gorges. Sometimes, when there came a big rain in the hills, the water would come down through the gorges and spread all over the farm. The last thing I remember of doing there was one Saturday afternoon; the other boys planted the corn in what we called the field — it contained seven acres — and I dropped the pumpkin seed. I dropped two seeds in every other row and every other hill. The next Sunday morning there came a big rain in the hills — it did not rain a drop in the valley, but the water, coming through the gorges, washed the ground, corn, pumpkin seeds and all, clear off the field! . . .

I can remember our life in Kentucky; the cabin, the stinted living, the sale of our possessions, and the journey with my father and mother to Southern Indiana. We removed to what is now Spencer County, Indiana, in the autumn of 1816, I then being in my eighth year. This removal was partly on account of slavery, but chiefly on account of the difficulty in land titles in Kentucky. . . .

Before leaving Kentucky, I and my sister [Sarah] were sent, for short periods, to A B C schools, the first kept by Zachariah Riney, the second by Caleb Hazel.

A three-year-old younger brother of Abraham is left behind in the ground as the Lincolns pull up stakes and move deeper into the wilderness, to uncleared land near Pigeon Creek, not far from Rockport, Indiana. To survive the first winter the father builds a "half-faced camp," a shed enclosed on three sides. There is no floor to cover the ground in the cabin, no oiled paper for the windows, no door for the doorway. The boy sleeps on a pile of dry leaves in a corner of the loft, got to by a ladder of pegs. He is nine, his sister Sarah eleven, when their mother dies of the milk-sick, which signals its coming with burning insides and a white coating of the tongue. Abraham helps his father build her coffin out of black cherry. It is the most dismal moment of Abe's young life when a horse pulls a sled with the coffin on it up a small hill a few hundred yards south of their cabin and Nancy Hanks Lincoln is laid to rest.

A year later the father makes his way back to Kentucky and wins the hand of a woman he had once courted — Sarah Bush Johnston (Sally, to some), now a widowed mother. For the forlorn and deserted Lincoln children, Sarah Bush is more than just a stepmother. She brings them not only three new playmates but also an abundance of warmth and affection. She dresses Abe in new clothes, encourages him to read and learn, chases the bleakness away and starts him on a new life.

"Sometimes he would write with a piece of charcoal," Dennis Hanks recalls, "or the p'int of a burnt stick, on the fence or floor. We got a little paper at the country town, and I made ink out of blackberry juice, briar root and a little copperas in it. It was black, but the copperas would eat the paper after a while. I made his first pen out of a turkey-buzzard feather. We hadn't no geese them days — to make good pens of goose quills."

Young Lincoln tries to understand the world around him. When there is something he can't comprehend, he doesn't simply put it out of mind.

Among my earliest recollections I remember how, when a mere child, I used to get irritated when anybody talked to me in a way that I could not understand. I can remember going to my little bedroom, after hearing the neighbors talk of an evening with my father, and spending no small part of the night trying to make out what was the exact meaning of some of their, to me, dark sayings.

I could not sleep, although I tried to, when I got on such a hunt for an idea, until I had caught it; and when I thought I had got it I was not satisfied until I had repeated it over and over again, until I had put it in language plain enough, as I thought, for any boy I knew to comprehend.

Along with the Bible, some classic fables and a few tales of far-off lands, Lincoln is learning some truths about his own young country.

Away back in my childhood, the earliest days of my being able to read, I got hold of a small book, [Mason Locke] Weems' *Life of Washington*. I remember all the accounts there given of the battlefields and struggles for the liberties of the country, and none fixed themselves upon my imagination so deeply as the struggle at Trenton, New Jersey. The crossing of the river, the contest with the Hessians, the great hardship endured at that time, all fixed themselves on my memory more than any single Revolutionary event. I recollect thinking then, boy even though I was, that there must have been something more than common that these men struggled for.

The spidery, spirited boy has become almost a celebrity among his peers because he can read and spell so well. As a young man now, he is showing a reflective quality in his thinking. Through reading, he is learning of a world outside of his immediate surroundings; he is learning what peoples did in distant lands in ages past; his eyes are suddenly opened to what law is and how governments work. Along with developing a certain amount of introspection, he is finding that the sound of his own voice isn't a bad sound at all — and it gets even better when he's making a point or telling a story. Now he's speaking on the stump, any stump he can find, to little groups of friends and neighbors; he's holding forth. Sometimes he's funny, sometimes serious. He goes to church on Sunday, and on Monday he repeats the sermon word for word, mimicking the preacher's every move.

At seventeen he does some ferry work on the rivers. At nineteen his sister dies trying to give birth to the child of her husband of three years. (It is said that the cause was a drunken doctor.) A few months later Abe heads down the Mississippi to New Orleans with a boat load of farm goods. He is big now, well over two hundred pounds, strong as a bear, an unbeatable wrestler. When the father decides to pull up stakes again — this time heading for Illinois — Abraham helps with the move, clearing the new land, splitting the rails for fences, and planting a first crop. Then he is ready to strike out on his own.

Leaving his desolate, hard, pioneer childhood behind, Lincoln again does river work on the Mississippi. In New Orleans he watches while a mulatto girl is paraded and prodded and pinched by prospective buyers as she is sold at auction. "If I ever get a chance to hit that institution," he says, "I'll hit it hard."

Back in Illinois Lincoln works in a store and a mill in New Salem, a boisterous little backwoods town he chooses as his new home. He borrows books from New Salem's educated families; he borrows a grammar book from Ann Rutledge, the pretty daughter of the tavern owner; he devours Thomas Paine and Shakespeare and Burns. He is appointed postmaster of primitive, brawling New Salem — not too taxing a job, since fewer than a hundred people live there and the mail arrives only once a week. His jokes and stories are often coarse — nothing delicate about this boy. With girls he is shy and acts the fool to cover up. He is poor. He does clerking work, legal assignments; he's a witness, he surveys. People can depend on him, people like him, he's quite the young man, fun to be with — this tall one with the fascinating face — people can rely on him.

He decides for politics, runs for the Illinois legislature, writes a campaign speech, gives it — loses. But he's on his way. He's kind of dreamy still, sometimes impractical, head a bit in the clouds. But he's sat down and actually written out a statement of his beliefs and what he'd do if he were elected. And his very first piece of political speech writing shows many of the qualities he will be known for later. He talks language everybody can understand. He sticks to subjects he knows. He's excited about "democracy" and the kind of great new society he sees it bringing upon the earth. Education is imperative, particularly reading. Reading has unlocked the doors of life for him, has allowed him to forswear what he views as the backbreaking, dead-end life of physical labor and enter instead the charmed life of the mind.

The young man's great lifelong devotions start to become clear: his fervor for the God of the Bible, for the Founding Fathers, for the Union, and for Democracy. But it is not enough for this pink-cheeked, amiable giant to keep his inchoate passions to himself. He wants to spread the word, share these ideas and gifts he so values. And more than anything, this big, bright, funny, honest, gangling, contemplative youth wants to be thought well of. "Every man is said to have his own particular ambition," he writes in that very first campaign speech. "I have no other so great as that of being truly esteemed of my fellow man, by rendering myself worthy of their esteem." This great drive to be honestly successful and deservedly respected will remain all-important through his entire life.

In the years that follow, Lincoln honors himself as a captain in the Black Hawk War; he runs again for the state legislature and this time wins; he begins to study law; and he undergoes a terrible sadness in the death of winsome, blue-eyed, auburn-haired Ann Rutledge, whom he joyfully loves and hopes to marry. For over a month after Ann dies of pneumonia, Lincoln disappears and loses himself in utter despair. It is more than a normal mourning over the death of a loved one. He is engulfed in an almost unbearable, irrational melancholy. Friends are afraid of suicide. Life has suddenly taken a bitter turn for which he has had little preparation. Something dark and indistinct seems to have him in its grip. "I ran off the track," Lincoln will admit toward the end of his life.

Finally he gets control of himself, puts his feet back on the ground, begins to function again. He is reelected to the legislature and he is licensed to practice law in Springfield, the new state capital, to which he moves. Politics in Springfield is rough-and-tumble, full of mudslinging between the Whigs — Lincoln's party — and the Democrats, with a lot of horseplay, parody, charges of dishonesty and of "dastardly" bargains; Lincoln loves it. He is a loner. He seldom offers praise. He frequents the general store and spins yarns around the fire. Politics is the talk of the day. He is uneasy with Springfield's fancy people; still, he is asked to their houses and their dances. He is an eligible bachelor about town.

He now reads legal briefs, philosophy, history, poetry. He has little interest in fiction or biography. He skims volumes, picking out what he wants, discarding the rest. And he is writing, sitting long hours with his pen, sifting through his thoughts and putting them down clearly and simply but with a ring to them that will get attention. It's not hard to know where this man's commitment lies: speaking in Vandalia, he refers to "the people" fourteen times in the space of two paragraphs. Lincoln is now twenty-seven years old — half the age he will be when he makes another, more notable speech far to the east in a little Pennsylvania town.

In January of 1838 Lincoln addresses the Young Men's Lyceum of Springfield. What he will say a quarter of a century later, he is already beginning to say now. His central concept is that the great task of the present generation is to uphold and preserve American democracy. His opening lines suggest the powerful and slightly distancing language of Ecclesiastes from the King James Old Testament. "In the great journal

OPPOSITE: *Some of the books Lincoln left behind in his law office when he departed for Washington in 1861 as President-elect*

of things happening under the sun," Lincoln begins in 1838. He goes on to echo Psalm 90, proclaiming: "The days of our years are three score and ten." Twenty-five years later his words will be even closer to their biblical antecedent — when he begins, "Four score and seven years ago. . . ."

Both speeches — one given almost at the start of Lincoln's career, the other almost at the finish — will use the term *proposition*, a word from the world of practical politics. In 1838 the underlying concept is "the capability of a people to govern themselves"; in 1863 it will be "that all men are created equal." Both are propositions that Lincoln believes in deeply; both require extraordinary vigilance to sustain.

In the 1838 speech, young Lincoln begins by locating himself and his Springfield audience in time — in history — by emphasizing the importance of remembering, lest the great deeds and accomplishments of the past be forgotten. And he voices the obligation to transfer the blessings of liberty and equal rights from one generation to the next. A national debt is owed to "the fathers"; the fading memory of the Revolution cannot be eroded by "the silent artillery of time." Twenty-five years later, at Gettysburg, Lincoln will weave his way between the distant past ("our fathers"), the immediate past ("what they did here"), the present

("Now we are engaged"), and a future ("the great task remaining before us"). Time will again be the crucial factor in his address.

Eighteen-forty is the year when Lincoln is becoming deeply involved with Mary Todd — Molly, as he calls her. The two have met at a cotillion in the autumn of 1839, and by the fall of the next year the flirtatious Southern belle with the quick mind and the saucy tongue has got the best of him; a wedding date is set for early 1841. But, unable to sort out his feelings and make such a momentous move, Lincoln abruptly calls off the engagement and once again retreats into mental and emotional anguish, a state that leaves him gaunt, unable to talk in a voice much above a whisper. "Crazy as a loon!" bellows Mary Todd's brother-in-law in disgust. Lincoln himself describes his melancholy condition as "hypochondriasm" and writes his friend Joshua Speed: "Whether I shall ever be better, I cannot tell; I awfully forbode I shall not. To remain as I am is impossible; I must die, or be better, it appears to me."

With the help of a running correspondence with Speed in Louisville, Kentucky, and then a visit to him, Lincoln gropes his way back to mental stability by sharing and dissecting and identifying with the thoughts and feelings of his friend, who has gone through a very similar emotional experience. In one of his letters Lincoln identifies his own worst problem: "I must regain my confidence in my own ability to keep my resolves when they are made. In that ability, you know, I once prided myself as the only, or at least the chief gem of my character; that gem I lost. . . . I have not yet regained it; and until I do, I cannot trust myself in any matter of much importance."

The following years are marked by Lincoln's revived relationship with Mary Todd, some interesting poetry he writes, the couple's subsequent marriage, a few memorable speeches he makes, and much hard work at his legal practice, both in Springfield and out on the circuit — expeditions he loves. These are trips on horseback (later taken in a one-horse carriage), often over roadless territory where small groups of

OPPOSITE: *From her home in Lexington, Kentucky, young, vivacious, well-educated Mary Ann Todd swept into Springfield in 1839 to visit her married sister and partake of the social life. Lincoln met her at a cotillion and was captivated. In 1842, after a tempestuous, off-and-on courtship, they were married. (This daguerreotype was taken four years later, probably by N. H. Shepherd. For reproduction here, the reversed daguerreotype image has been re-reversed to show the true appearance of Mrs. Lincoln's features.)*

lawyers and judges have to ford streams and sometimes bushwhack to get to their distant destinations.

The years on the circuit toughen Lincoln, make him understand people better, make him see their strengths and foibles more clearly. From county seat to county seat he and his colleagues move, stopping for whatever time is necessary to try cases: prosecuting, defending, passing judgments, issuing fines and sentences, and then moving on, leaving behind their special brand of American justice. Lincoln enjoys being away from the responsibilities of his Springfield office and his duties as a father and a husband. He does not hurry home. He is with "the people."

Often he shares a bed with a fellow lawyer at the local tavern, and evenings are spent trading tall stories. The people line up to listen, urge

In a string of understanding letters, best friend Joshua Speed helped steer Lincoln toward marriage by calming his anguish. (This picture was taken by Mathew Brady twenty years later.)

the visitors on, and join in the side-splitting laughter. When there is an "entertainment" in town, a traveling circus or a magician's performance, Lincoln mysteriously disappears; it is a distinguished lot of men he travels with and comes up against in court. Lincoln is at his best as a lawyer at home, when he has plenty of time to do his research and think his cases through and through, but still, even in these primitive settings, he is formidable. Over the years he earns respect and gains a reputation wherever he goes. Honor and distinction are just what he has always been seeking.

At home in Springfield it is a fairly relaxed life, with none of the hurried bustle of a big city. Lincoln has become a sort of pet of the town — admired, made over, listened to, praised. He and Mary have bought a house at the corner of Eighth and Jackson streets. He is often seen at the grocery store with a market basket on his arm; he will take on all comers at chess or checkers; he plays stickball and tenpins with the neighborhood children; he pulls his own little ones around the streets in a toy wagon; he cares for his cow, curries his horse, romps with his dog. Everybody knows the tall, slightly pigeon-toed man with the slow,

The Lincoln's dog Fido

deliberate step who carries his hands clasped behind his back. Everybody knows his voice as, passing by, he calls, "Howdy, howdy."

As time goes on the Lincolns hardly ever entertain. Now Lincoln doesn't even bring his best friends home for dinner. Mary has become erratic and high-strung. At the onset of a thunderstorm Lincoln can be seen loping home from his office to comfort his terrified wife. Over the years Mary will become known less and less for her wit and beauty and more and more for her odd, cranky behavior and her sudden bursts of

Detail from the first known photograph of Lincoln, probably taken by N. H. Shepherd in Springfield. Lincoln was thirty-seven years old at the time and had recently been elected to the United States Congress. (The reversed daguerreotype image has been re-reversed here.)

temper. Lincoln sometimes just laughs at her. But Mary, in her anger, will even resort to a club or a knife, and then Lincoln will retreat to his office. He will not retaliate. Rather, he becomes cool and removed. Still, he can joke: No, he will not lend out his buggy. There are two things in this world he will not lend to anyone on earth — his wife and his buggy.

In 1846 Lincoln is elected to the U.S. House of Representatives. In Washington he makes himself heard on the war with Mexico, claiming that the United States has no right to invade its southern neighbor and openly criticizing President James Polk: "He does not know where he is. He is a bewildered, confounded and miserably perplexed man." Such open opposition to a President in time of war is not popular, and Lincoln is criticized both in the capital and back home in Illinois. It makes little difference that he is speaking out of his commitment to the truth and what he feels is morally correct for the country.

In the summer and fall of 1848 Congressman Lincoln actively campaigns for the Whig presidential candidate, General Zachary Taylor. In September Lincoln and his family leave on a speaking tour of New England. Lincoln gives his first widely respected speech at the city hall in Worcester, Massachusetts. The *Boston Daily Advertiser* reviews his appearance: "He has a very tall and thin figure, with an intellectual face, showing a searching mind and cool judgment. He spoke in a clear and cool and very eloquent manner for an hour and a half."

From Worcester Lincoln goes on to successful stops in New Bedford, Boston, Lowell, Dorchester, Chelsea, Dedham, Cambridge, Taunton, and again at Boston, before returning home to Illinois. In November General Taylor is elected President.

Having sacrificed continuation in Congress by an election promise, Lincoln now undertakes a massive effort to secure an appointment for himself as commissioner of the General Land Office. When someone else is granted the position, Lincoln once again sinks into despondence, self-doubt, and confusion. It is Mary Todd Lincoln who keeps the belief in a great destiny for her husband alive. Tempted by the office of the governorship of the Oregon Territory, which seems to him a way out of his troubles, Lincoln turns it down at the insistence of his wife.

Feeling that he has failed in politics, Lincoln now devotes himself tirelessly to law and to study. When he is not out on the circuit he spends his evenings devouring law books, books on mathematics and logic, Euclid's great works. During these years Lincoln's powers of logic and argument are enlarged and reinforced. In the early mornings he turns to literature, studying again Shakespeare, Byron, Burns: skimming here, memorizing there, dipping in and out of quantities of books rather than reading any one through from beginning to end. Now Lincoln's mind seems to shed its earlier romanticism and take on a harshness more consistent with the events of the world.

Then, finally, the issue that will consume Lincoln for the rest of his life is before him. On May 30, 1854, President Franklin Pierce signs the controversial Kansas-Nebraska Act, canceling out the work of the Missouri Compromise and opening up a great portion of the Louisiana Purchase to slavery. The bill's designer and chief advocate is Stephen A. Douglas — U.S. senator from Illinois, close acquaintance of Lincoln, fellow Springfield lawyer, former suitor for the hand of Mary Todd. In October of 1854, at forty-five, Lincoln is called upon to reply to Douglas and does so at Peoria in a speech that deals with the subject of slavery on a whole new plane of vision. Gone is the vagueness of the previous years. Gone are Lincoln's old romantic displays of metaphor and personal theology. He has finally found what his capabilities longed for: a cause large enough and worthy enough to devote his highest efforts to — all his keenness of mind; his knowledge of government, law, and American history; his sense of morality; his dedication to God; and his love of country. The nation has been arguing over slavery for decades; now it suddenly has gained a clear champion against all slavery, who, if not determined to fight it where it already exists, is at least firm in his resolve not to let its unspeakable unfairness — its "monstrous injustice," as he now calls it — creep into the huge territories of the Middle West.

Almost overnight the Peoria speech makes Lincoln famous. Encouraged by this powerful success, he enters the senatorial race and almost wins. A year and a half later he receives 110 convention votes for vice-president on General John C. Frémont's ticket. Then, in early 1857, under James Buchanan's presidency, the Supreme Court hands down its momentous Dred Scott decision, which basically denies citizenship to all Negroes. The justices state that Negroes are "so far inferior

Dred Scott, the slave who claimed to be free and provoked the Supreme Court, in 1857, to deny citizenship to all Negroes. (Reproduced from a copy of a photograph belonging to a grand-niece of Dred Scott's one-time owner.)

Just before Alexander Hesler exposed this 1857 portrait in Chicago, Lincoln ran his hand through his hair. He wanted to make sure his friends would recognize him, he said.

that they had no rights which the white man was bound to respect," that the "all created equal" clause of the Declaration of Independence does not refer to Negroes, and that the word *citizen* in the Constitution cannot include Negroes — slave or free. The democratic experiment is coming apart. A head-on eruption between the forces of the Southern slave-owning states and the Northern abolitionist states, although not yet inevitable, seems a distinct possibility.

In June of 1857 both Douglas and Lincoln give speeches concerning the Supreme Court decision. First Douglas argues for popular sovereignty in the new territories and interprets the clause "all men are created equal" from the Declaration of Independence as a reference "to the white race alone, and not to the African." Lincoln believes the decision by the predominately Southern justices is wrong. He sees terrible dangers being set loose if the Declaration of Independence is to be reinterpreted so. Not that Lincoln advocates racial intermixture: he, like Douglas and most white American thinkers of his day, considers himself clearly superior to all Negroes. That is a matter of intellectual or "natural" inequality. But he insists upon legal equality for them, for he believes that's what had been envisioned in the Declaration of Independence. The "all created equal" clause, he argues, had been inserted there precisely to urge the new nation to take the slavery question seriously and work toward the institution's eventual elimination. "They meant to declare the *right*, so that the enforcement of it might follow as fast as circumstances should permit."

Between June and November of 1858, Lincoln gives more than sixty speeches on this subject. He begins on June 16 in Springfield with his great speech about a house divided. "I believe this government cannot endure, permanently half slave and half free." In July, speaking in Chicago, Lincoln goes on the record in favor of not only confining slavery to its present states but also insuring its ultimate extinction. Here he also demonstrates the Founders' full intention to abolish slavery, as an evil. In August, in Lewistown, he continues his argument about the intentions of the Founding Fathers: "In their enlightened belief, nothing stamped with the Divine Image and likeness was sent into the world to be trodden on, and degraded, and imbruted by its fellows." In October he notes: "As a *good* thing, slavery is strikingly peculiar, in . . . that it is the only good thing which no man ever seeks the good of, for *himself*. Nonsense! Wolves devouring lambs, not because it is good for their own greedy maws, but because it [is] good for the lambs!!!"

As Lincoln and Douglas meet head-on in debate, the questions each present to the other become sharpened, more refined. Douglas continues to avoid involving himself in Lincoln's charge of conspiracy, refusing to "go into that beautiful figure of his about the building of a house." The fulcrum of the debates swings around the "all created equal" clause of the Declaration and the question of slavery.

Lincoln hammers away: "[Douglas] looks upon [slavery] as being an exceedingly little thing . . . as something having no moral question in it. . . . It so happens that there is a vast portion of the American people that . . . look upon it as a vast moral evil."

And again: "I should like to know if taking this old Declaration of Independence, which declares that all men are created equal upon principle, and making exceptions to it, where will it stop. If one man says it does not mean a negro, why not another say it does not mean some other man?"

And again: "I charge him [Douglas] with having been a party to that conspiracy and to that deception, for the sole purpose of nationalizing slavery."

When the news reaches Douglas in Washington that Lincoln has been nominated to be his opponent in the 1858 race for his Senate seat, the Little Giant knows what he is up against. "I shall have my hands full," he says. "He is the strong man of his party — full of wits, facts,

Stephen A. Douglas, senator from Illinois, debated Lincoln on the subject of slavery over and over in 1858. (A broken glass negative by Brady was pieced together to make this image.)

This ambrotype made by Calvin Jackson on October 1, 1858, shows how Lincoln looked just before the fifth debate with Douglas. Two weeks earlier Douglas had flatly stated: "This government . . . was made by white men, for the benefit of white men . . . and never should be administered by any except white men."

dates — and the best stump speaker, with his droll ways and dry looks, in the West. He is as honest as he is shrewd and if I beat him my victory will be hardly won."

Douglas does beat Lincoln for the Senate seat and years later Lincoln will tell John Hay how he felt walking home that night: "The path had been worn pig-backed and was slippery. My foot slipped from under me, knocking the other out of the way; but I recovered and said to myself, 'It's a slip and not a fall.'" The slip has helped earn Lincoln a national reputation. As a consequence, in May of 1860 Lincoln gains the nomination of the Republican party as its candidate for President of the United States. The country is stunned by the choice, not least of all the citizens of Springfield, who can hardly believe that their noted local lawyer has suddenly been catapulted into the possible leadership of the whole nation.

Springfield's cannon roars its first ear-splitting blast, salute number one of a hundred that are being fired off in honor of the father of the two boys who are trying obediently to keep quiet in the prim parlor of their house. Tad and Willie's lives are suddenly, irrevocably changed. At each deafening explosion the windows in the house rattle as though they are about to fall out of their frames. A crowd of neighbors appears out of nowhere. They have come to tell the boys' mother that Mr. Lincoln has been nominated to be President of the United States. Now they have told her and she is standing in the middle of the waving, shouting, jumping men and women. Suddenly Tad and Willie find themselves beside her, yelling too, and being knocked and jostled about for all they are worth.

Just at that moment everyone looks down the street to see a curious, angular, loose-boned figure flying homeward toward them — his coat-tails flapping out behind him, his black rumpled hair on end, his dark face alight. Lincoln has left the telegraph office the minute they hand him the slip of paper with the message on it: MR. LINCOLN, YOU ARE NOMINATED ON THE THIRD BALLOT. "Excuse me," he says, as he goes out the door, "but there's a little woman down at our house who will be interested in this."

The boys make a dash for their father. Willie hangs from Lincoln's left arm with his feet off the ground, kicking in excitement like a furious centipede. Tad simply climbs up his tall father as if he were a tree — shinnies up him and hugs him in a stranglehold around the neck. Explosions continue to rend the air with frightening loudness. People begin to push and shove to reach Lincoln's hand and pump it up and down.

Soon bells begin to ring out from church towers, some deep and some high voiced. Flags are hung from houses all over the town. Groups of men hurry off to get their rifles and set up private shooting parties so that the confusion will not die down when the cannon has completed its stint. Like a battle, it all sounds, except that the cries of the voices are joyful and friendly.

As night begins to fall the whole town of Springfield comes to the Lincoln doorstep, and everyone who can squeeze in comes into the Lincoln house. People march with torches in their hands and fence rails on their shoulders, raising unending cheers for Old Abe. Firecrackers are set off, and later on, skyrockets. Up and down the street crackle the huge fires of burning tar barrels, and spaced between them blaze great bonfires — for the most part built and tended by the town's small boys. Armies of them have spent the afternoon collecting old boxes and wooden junk of every variety. They have even commandeered amounts of perfectly good kindling that represented hours of some chopper's work. They have also cleared the woods of vast quantities of dry underbrush, moving what looks like mountains of sticks and branches to the vicinity of the Lincoln house. The heat of the fires is terrific and they burn long into the night as Lincoln regales his guests with story after story. What a night it has been for Springfield; for Illinois; for the West! What a night it has been for the Lincolns!

All through the next day the church bells continue to peal and citizens stand about in little gatherings to discuss the honor that has been done them. Even the horses wear little flags in their harnesses. At eight o'clock that night the official notification committee arrives at the Lincoln doorstep and is ushered inside. Against Mrs. Lincoln's wishes, ice water is served instead of champagne; the nervous nominee feels he cannot afford to make a mistake and that water is less likely to offend than alcohol. During the ensuing ceremony, Lincoln stands at the east end of his parlor, the committee facing him at a distance. Tad and

OPPOSITE: *In the summer of 1860, a little more than a month after his nomination, Lincoln (standing just to the right of the doorway) donned a white suit and posed in front of his house in the midst of joyous celebration.*

Willie are in the hall, where they can both see and hear what is going on. Congressman George Ashmun, the chairman, begins to speak.

"I have, sir, the honor, in behalf of the gentlemen who are present, a committee appointed by the Republican Convention recently assembled at Chicago, to discharge a most pleasant duty. We have come, sir, under a vote of instructions to that Committee, to notify you that you have been selected by the Convention of the Republicans at Chicago, for President of the United States."

But strangely, Lincoln is not looking at the moment like a President at all. He is not even looking at the notification committee or Mr. Ashmun. He is standing instead with eyes downcast and shoulders sloped forward, seemingly a man dejected to the point of despair. There is something wooden about his face, with its hollows and its deep, graven lines. He looks undecided. He does not look like a great man at all. The sight does not help the confidence of Lincoln's friends who are crowded into the room. Hardly a man or a woman in that solemn group is completely confident that the perfect person — or even the best available — has been chosen to lead the nation. That Lincoln is honest they know. But the country has been run over with talk about the man's coarseness, his uncouthness, his ugliness, his lack of formal education. He has been called everything from a third-rate country lawyer to a gorilla. What he stands for they well know: the Union — and against slavery as a moral wrong. That is good; but one and all, in their hearts, they fear for the government now that it is to be placed in such untried, such humble and inexpert hands.

Mr. Ashmun finishes his speech, and Lincoln then replies.

Mr. Chairman, and Gentlemen of the Committee, and all the people represented in it, my profoundest thanks for the high honor done me, which you now formally announce. Deeply, and even painfully sensible of the great responsibility which is inseparable from this high honor — a responsibility

*President-elect
Lincoln visited his
adored stepmother
Sally for the last time
before going east.
(His father had
died in 1851.)*

which I could almost wish had fallen upon some one of the far more eminent men and experienced statesmen whose distinguished names were before the Convention, I shall, by your leave, consider more fully the resolutions of the Convention, denominate the platform, and without unreasonable delay, respond to you, Mr. Chairman, in writing, not doubting that the platform will be found satisfactory and the nomination gratefully accepted.

And now, I will not longer defer the pleasure of taking you, and each one of you, by the hand.

All present are confounded and rejoice at what they see. For as Lincoln utters his first word, his tall figure straightens up to its full height, his whole bearing speaks of dignity and great strength held in tight leash within the man; his eyes light and his whole face moves into an entirely new expression as though the features have been instantaneously molded anew. It is this mobile quality of Lincoln's face that the people close to him will come to know so well over the next years, a quality no photograph is able to convey: his expressions are too fleeting and their shadings too subtle and myriad.

This is how Lincoln looked in the summer of 1860 in an ambrotype made by Preston Butler. It was only a few months before his election and the beard that would soon follow.

TEN

GETTYSBURG came alive early on the morning of November 19, 1863. Before dawn the roads and turnpikes leading toward the town had already begun to fill. Horse-drawn vehicles of every description — from Conestoga wagons and buggies to carriages, ambulances, and carts — were joined by hundreds of early-rising citizens on foot. By the time the sun finally peeked over the still-green hills to the east on this hazy, brisk Thursday morning, the spokelike arteries leading to Gettysburg were ribboned with humanity on the move, all headed in the same direction and for the same purpose. The trains were still coming in too, packed to the hilt, standing room only; and when all these new arrivals joined up with Gettysburg's regular citizens and the thousands who had been pouring in all week long, there was hardly any room to turn around or air to breathe in the town's few narrow streets.

At exactly 7:00 A.M. thundering salvos were fired from Cemetery Hill to mark the official beginning of this day to be remembered. People not already awake sat up fast now and drew on their boots, shoehorning their feet swollen from all that walking the night before, clearing their throats from all that singing. Women excitedly tied their bone corsets, pulled up high stockings, arranged the hoops of their skirts. The smells of breakfast drifted across the town — the aroma of coffee and bacon mixed with the woodsmoke from hundreds of iron stoves. Plates were left in the sink this morning; everyone was in a hurry to get out of doors and join in the commotion that already seemed to have reached fever pitch. Everywhere musical instruments were being tuned and tooted: clarinets squealed and tubas belched as scales were climbed and lips tested; drumsticks made a hundred dizzy rolls against taught skins; the heartthrob of a bass drum signaled the center of a band. Marchers and musicians left the top buttons of their uniforms loose and carried their hats as if to announce that the time had not yet come to form up and look perfect.

The dew dried and now dust from the streets began to rise, giving a hazier cast to everything. Dogs barked, chased each other in and out among all the feet; horses were brought up and they sneezed in the haze, shook their heads, whinnied and stomped as they waited for things to get under way. Everyone had something to say. Orders flew. People spotted friends and there were hugs and pushings through the crowd and slaps on the back. The trains continued to unload their passengers and the carriages kept coming too. Not a window along all of Baltimore Street was not packed with spectators who'd staked out their positions days before.

Everyone remembered something different about the morning, especially where the President was concerned. One of Lincoln's suggested travel plans had called for two hours of battlefield inspection early

Thursday morning; his final official plan left that out. Still, Seward much later claimed that he and Lincoln had visited the grounds of the seminary in a buckboard during early hours; and the Honorable William Mc-Dougall of Canada, one of the guests on Lincoln's train the day before, went even further, saying that he had driven to the battlefields that morning with the President and that Lincoln had been "solemn and absorbed" at the sights he beheld. Memory of that day was not to be trusted, especially after the event had taken on special importance and participants were trying to enhance history's remembrance of their own involvement. Neither Lincoln's secretaries nor any newspapermen on the scene reported any such trip to the battlefields.

John Nicolay went to Lincoln's room at the Wills house at 9:00 A.M. He later remembered sitting there while Lincoln made a new copy of his address; according to Nicolay, the President crossed things out as he copied and inserted some last thoughts. Also at 9:00 A.M., James A. Rebert, Company B, Twenty-first Pennsylvania Cavalry, reported to the room as Lincoln's orderly for the day. Just before ten o'clock, Lincoln made a roll of the two pages of writing he planned to deliver and tucked them into his coat pocket. Then he rose, put on his high hat, tugged white gauntlets over his hands, and went downstairs to join the procession that had been assembling below his window for over an hour.

The Wills house had been a refuge; now, as Lincoln emerged from its front door, he was assaulted by noise and movement and color. Dress of the day for all marshals called for black suit, black hat, white gloves, white satin sash, red-white-and-blue rosette on left breast, and white saddlecloth bordered with black. Along with the fancy dress uniforms of the military, the marshals' costumes gave the assembling paraders a dashing, circus look. Wills had written Chief Marshal Lamon that he had scraped together a hundred horses — "such as they are" — for use in the procession. The marshals had already picked up their steeds from the quartermaster, and now they were trying them out all about the square. At the doorway of the Wills house, Lincoln put his hand around the shoulder of Governor Curtin's twelve-year-old son and gave a squeeze.

Two tight lines of soldiers had formed an aisle from the Willses' doorstep out onto the crowded Diamond — a human channel leading to a small bay horse, saddled and ready. This was to be the President's loco-motion for the day, but whoever had done the choosing of horseflesh had not reckoned with Lincoln's size. Waving, he passed through the corridor of soldiers and the cloudburst of cheers that his appearance had brought forth. But now, as he swung himself up onto his steed, his legs hung much too low to the ground for a Commander in Chief. He should have been seated on an enormous, fiery charger with smoke in its nostrils and prance in its hoof, not on a calm little horse that took virtually no guid-ing at all, that didn't even start at the sound of a cannon salvo, that was so pitifully short the President's feet practically dragged on the ground. Everybody, it seemed, was trying to shake Lincoln's hand or, failing that, at least touch him in some way. Small horse or not, he did look imposing, with that black suit and his high black hat with the mourning band wrapped around its stovepipe.

Chief Marshal Lamon was trying to arrange the paraders in proper order. He and his seventy-two marshals with bright sashes stretched across their chests galloped about, giving orders, trying to get the four military bands to stop their tooting and socializing and prepare for busi-ness. Try as they might, nobody seemed to be responding — neither the dignitaries nor the soldiers, the governors nor the mayors, and certainly not the fire departments, the Knights Templar, the Odd Fellows, and the just plain citizens who were to bring up the rear.

For a full hour Lincoln sat patiently on the puny bay, taking hands when they were thrust at him, nodding and smiling, chatting when he could be heard. At one point during the hubbub, Governor Curtin was able to make some remarks to the President. He told him about a serenade that had been given Governor Horatio Seymour of New York the night before. "He deserves it," Lincoln responded. "No man has shown greater interest and promptness in his cooperation with us."

If Lincoln's spirits needed raising, they got a good lift when a telegram from Secretary of War Stanton in Washington was handed to him. It informed the President that General Grant had wired that "Sherman's movement had commenced and that a battle or falling back of enemy by Saturday at the farthest is inevitable." There was also an update on Tad: "Mrs. Lincoln reports your son's health a great deal better and he will be out today." Lincoln read the message and smiled and read it again and thanked the soldier who had brought it.

Time passed; the morning was almost gone. Suddenly the crowd that had filled the Diamond gave way and began surging up Baltimore, the main street, and toward the battlefields beyond. It was only half a mile to the cemetery, and people had decided to give up on the procession and find good positions for the ceremonies. They also wanted to get a look at some of the famous spots they had read so much about in the papers: Culp's Hill, Seminary Ridge, Little Round Top, Cemetery Ridge, the Peach Orchard, Devil's Den, the Wheat-Field. At eleven o'clock, when the parade was finally ready to move (one hour behind schedule), it had lost at least half of its citizen marchers and many of its street-side admirers because of the long delay.

To the thud of bass drums and the smart blast of brass, the procession began to weave out of the Diamond and onto the street, making its way along Baltimore toward the Emmitsburg road, where it would branch right, then turn left onto the Taneytown road and climb the hill to the cemetery.

Out front with knees high and in perfect step came the color guard and Marine band, followed by the official military delegation: the Second United States Artillery; the U.S. Regular Cavalry; Major General Couch and staff; Major General Julius Stahel and staff; the Twentieth Pennsyl-

vania Cavalry; Colonel Charles M. Provost and staff; Battery A, Fifth U.S. Regulars; Major General Schenck and staff; and the band of the Fifth New York Heavy Artillery Regiment. The day would have been more perfect, of course, if General Meade had been there — the man responsible for the great Gettysburg victory, the current commander of the Army of the Potomac. Meade had received an invitation, extended not only to himself but to his troops as well. He had declined for them all, officers and privates alike — "who stood side by side in the struggle," Meade had written David Wills; they "shared the peril, and the vacant places in those ranks bear sad testimony to the loss they have sustained." Duty called, Meade explained. "This army has duties to perform which will not permit of being represented on the occasion." Semiretired, gout-ridden, former General-in-Chief Winfield Scott declined as well, as did Lincoln's secretary of war and his secretary of the navy. In many ways it was an unexceptional turnout.

Every minute along the way a cannon shot resounded. The music from the bands was slow: dirges for the dead. Faces were solemn. The pace was funereal. Flags were supposed to fly at half-mast until noon. Windows were hung in black. Following the military came the President and the attending cabinet members, escorted by Chief Marshal Lamon and his top aides. Seward and Blair rode on Lincoln's right, Usher and Lamon on his left; just behind rode Nicolay and Hay. More generals followed, then governors and commissioners of participating states and various other honored guests, and finally the civic divisions: the U.S. Sanitary Commission, lodge members, city councils, faculty and students from the local seminary and college, and, at last, "the people" — just plain, ordinary, unattached citizens.

Lincoln swayed loosely from one side of his horse to the other, at first waving, responding to the cheers, but finally in a kind of daze, as if he were lost in faraway thoughts. Alongside him, Seward was more attentive to his mount; horses and the secretary of state were almost complete strangers, and the President's adviser looked awkward, a bit nervous, as he clumped along, his trouser legs working farther and farther up his leg and showing more and more of his gray socks. Along the route a young girl dressed in her party best was thrust upon the President. He took her gently and gave her a short ride perched in front of him before planting a kiss on her forehead and handing her back to her pleased parent. At another point an officer's horse became overly interested in the tail of Lincoln's bay and had to be restrained from repeatedly nipping at it.

Less than five months ago, the land here, the houses, the trees had been mercilessly violated. Lincoln could see the evidence as he rode by: bullet holes embedded in the walls of buildings; splintered trees cut in half; children at little stands along the way selling shell fragments as if they were rare minerals. For those three days in July a volcano had exploded, leaving its ash, its rock, its refuse behind. Birds had disappeared, rabbits had fled, squirrels and chipmunks had escaped to the next county. Even the termites seemed to have stopped work on the fence posts. It was killing time.

Now the bloated, reeking, fly-infested corpses of ten thousand steeds stiff in death and punctured by returning vultures rotted in the orchards, poisoning the air. Throughout the fields of wheat and corn, across the orchards, over the hillsides, amid the trees — everywhere was the evidence of death: a shoe here, a belt buckle there, a dented canteen, a tattered vest, a torn picture of a child — scraps of men's lives scattered to the winds. The men themselves were no more than mounds in the earth now, mounds with wooden markers and penciled epitaphs upon them — inscriptions bleached by the sun, washed by the rain, hardly visible anymore: name, rank, unit.

A slight fog, perhaps merely the haze of the road dust, enshrouded the town as the procession moved up the gentle rise of Baltimore Street and then descended to the outskirts of the town. Groups of spectators —

OPPOSITE: *Dead horses were still rotting in the fields and orchards. Here carcasses lie beside Trostle's barn, where heavy fighting took place.*

a few on horseback, some in buggies, most on foot — mingled in the middle of the wide dirt road and off to its sides, under trees, beside fences, in front of the neat residences, waiting for the slow beat of the drums and the plaintive music of the bands. When the spectators along the way spotted the procession coming, women waved from second-story porches, children balanced themselves on fence rails, and everyone strained his neck to catch a glimpse of the President.

Lincoln was slumping forward now, still swaying as he rode, paying no attention at all to the rest of the procession. And there, behind, just to make sure that this was not a day of rejoicing for all these spectators — just to keep everyone's mind on the business at hand — was a block of forty soldiers who had been wounded in the July fighting. Many of them were still bandaged from their stay at the military hospital thirty miles away at York. Many limped along on crutches. Many had arm slings. They were the lucky ones, marching today to pay homage to their fallen comrades.

ELEVEN

LINCOLN knew all the details of the great battle; he had studied the terrain on maps, read the military telegrams that had come in, was familiar with the commanding officers. During the fighting he had kept abreast of all the major decisions. Now, swaying back and forth on his little brown horse, lost in thought, Lincoln could conjure up what had happened on these roads, in these fields, up these hills, among these quiet trees. He could almost feel the intense heat of those three horrific days in July, almost hear the guns and the yells of men, almost smell the acrid powder-smoke, almost see the dead to whom he had come to pay tribute.

It had all started so casually, as if by accident, just four months and nineteen days ago. The two great enemy armies had been moving about the Maryland and Pennsylvania countryside, each knowing the other was out in the hills somewhere, but not knowing exactly where. On

Monday, June 29, the weekly issue of the *Gettysburg Compiler* had contained an advertisement for men's boots and shoes available at the Gettysburg store of R. F. McIlheny. Camped nearby, Confederate Major General Henry Heth either read or heard about the sale and on Wednesday, July 1, he marched a brigade into town to collect some footwear for his men, who were sadly in need of new shodding after their long march north. For two and a half years now the war in the East had been taking place over a relatively small area in Maryland and Virginia — the same homely names of cities, towns, villages, depots, crossings, streams, bridges, and landings cropping up again and again as the scenes of conflict. Now a full-fledged invasion of the North by the Confederates was in the offing, a bold move that might rapidly alter the standoff complexion of the war.

A few miles west of town, General Heth's infantry ran into some Union cavalry scouts stationed at Gettysburg under the command of General John Buford. There was scattered firing. Things quieted, then suddenly picked up again with some more firing. This time the fighting was fiercer. More and more soldiers joined in. And once the skirmish got big enough, there was no stopping it. The battle of Gettysburg had begun.

In early June, just a month before, the Confederate Army of Northern Virginia was riding high. It had recently come off its greatest victory so far — at the crossroads of Chancellorsville, where General Robert E. Lee and an army only half the size of the Federals repulsed General Joseph Hooker's drive into Virginia. Things were not as good for the Confederacy in the Mississippi Valley, where General Grant had Vicksburg under attack; one Southern proposal in June was that Lee be sent to Tennessee to head an offensive there that would ultimately force the North to withdraw Grant from his siege. But Lee had, he thought, a better idea. Even though his army was depleted and he had lost the brilliant Stonewall Jackson at Chancellorsville, he began moving his army of seventy thousand men north toward the Potomac River, the borderline between Rebel and Yankee territory. The Army of the Potomac lay between him and Washington, effectively preventing a direct attack upon the city. Lee's plan was to drive into Maryland and Pennsylvania, march eastward above Hooker's army, and then, in a great surprise attack, descend upon Washington from the north. If Hooker discovered his plan and pursued, then Lee would attack the northern cities of Harrisburg and Philadelphia, turning upon and defeating the Union army when the time was right, and then proceeding on to undefended Washington. Southern morale was high, the Army of Northern Virginia considered itself unbeatable, and General Robert E. Lee hoped his audacious plan would win the Second American Revolution.

But from the beginning, things went wrong for Lee. For one, he lost contact with his cavalry scouts under Major General Jeb Stuart; without their surveillance, Lee no longer had a continuous line on the position of the enemy. Stuart got trapped east of the Army of the Potomac and could not get back to Lee until late in the second day of fighting at Gettysburg. Then, in addition, Lee assumed that Hooker and the Yankees knew nothing of his plans, for the march northward was taking place to the west of the Blue Ridge, out of sight of Hooker's surveillance. Lee hoped that his invasion of Yankee territory would not be discovered until it was too late; however, a cavalry run-in on June 9 at Brandy Station, south of the Rappahannock River in Virginia, changed all that. Among Southern papers seized that day by Union soldiers were Lee's orders to Stuart, describing his plans for an invasion of the North. Thus, in a matter of days after Lee had started northward, Hooker was following with close to a hundred thousand men.

Working against Lee as well was a sudden change in the command of the Army of the Potomac at the end of June. At Chancellorsville Lee had discovered to his delight what he could do to the erratic Fighting Joe Hooker, who could not take the pressures of high command in a battle situation. Hooker's successor, Major General George Gordon Meade, could. Meade might have been like a "damned goggle-eyed snapping turtle" in temperament — an expression he overheard one of his men use to describe him — but he wasn't scared of anything, certainly not of being in command or the reputation of Robert E. Lee.

Lee, deprived of his "eyes" by Jeb Stuart's absence and lulled into a false security about the position of the Army of the Potomac, had fanned his army out over the Pennsylvania countryside in a forty-five-mile-long crescent. Then, on the evening of June 28, luck finally rode with him. Information was received by Lee from a Confederate spy that Meade had not only taken over the Union command but that the Army of the Potomac was at that very moment amassed near Frederick, Maryland, only twenty miles from the Pennsylvania border. Confederate couriers galloped the roads that night, from Chambersburg to Harrisburg to York, calling in the Southern generals and their men. All would meet in the convenient little Pennsylvania town of Gettysburg, from which so many roads radiated.

Lumbering northward, feeling for the enemy, not really knowing where Johnny Reb was but picking out a logical possibility on the map, the Army of the Potomac in turn was heading for the Pennsylvania border, aiming for the same little town where all the roads met.

For no particular reason except that Gettysburg was there and central and the hub of many arteries, the location of the most crucial battle of the Civil War had been selected.

Day one, July 1: In the opening skirmish, General Heth is easily overpowering Buford's cavalry when Federal reinforcements arrive. The Union's famous Iron Brigade, made up of well-trained, hard-fighting westerners, marches through Gettysburg and out to meet the enemy, joined on its way by a seventy-year-old Gettysburg cobbler named John

Burns. Burns is to receive three wounds that day, but will live and become a local hero. The battle doubles in size, triples. The fighting becomes intense. But at this point neither Lee, in the mountains to the west, nor Meade, in the hills to the south, is ready to provoke a full-scale battle. Lee is still waiting for all his men to gather and Meade is not yet sure where Lee's men are mustering. The fighting just to the west of Gettysburg increases.

At noon Federal reinforcements stream through the town after a long forced march and are greeted by wild cheers from the Gettysburg citizens, along with offerings of bread, apple butter, and cold water. Gettysburg women have been watching the battle all morning from the upper porches and windows of their houses. The fighting has become furious now, involving thousands of men on each side. The Confederate army's great crescent above the town is pushing the Union army backward.

At three o'clock additional Confederate troops arrive from the northeast and strike at the Federal flank. The battle turns into a rout: Federal troops stream back through the town, running south for Cemetery Hill, where there are reinforcements. All order has broken down as the retreat turns wild. Many Gettysburg women open their doors to Union soldiers, taking them into their cellars. Already the public buildings of the town — the hotels, the taverns, the churches, the schools, the courthouse — are being converted into makeshift hospitals and are filling with the wounded. As panic grows in the Federal ranks, the scene is set for a swift and decisive Confederate victory.

But the stars turn against Lee. For on this day and the two to follow, hesitation and misunderstanding plague him and his commanders.

The first and most disastrous of Lee's lost opportunities occurs this first afternoon. Communication between Lee and Lieutenant General Richard Ewell, who is commanding the Second Corps, is terrible. Ewell, trained under Stonewall Jackson, is accustomed to direct, explicit orders.

Lee, on the other hand, prefers to leave his divisional commanders room for improvisation. At noon Ewell receives these words from Lee: "A general engagement should be avoided if possible." All afternoon Ewell worries about those two words *if possible*. By three, during the rout, it becomes clear to Lee that if Ewell were to strike Cemetery Hill before the Union soldiers can secure it, the day would be the Confederates'. Ewell's own officers urge him to mount a full attack on the hill. Then Lee's second message to Ewell arrives: "Press those people in order to secure possession of the heights, if it is possible."

Those four confusing last words! Ewell cannot deal with this kind of an order. He becomes indecisive and absentminded, and despite persistent urgings from his outraged officers, he decides simply to do nothing. At about four-thirty that afternoon Ewell sits down to tea with the ladies of the Blocker farmhouse.

Now an attack on Cemetery Ridge is impractical, for sundown approaches. Nor will it be possible the next morning, Lee knows; his entire offensive will have to be switched to the Union left. The Confederates withdraw for the night and both sides tend their wounded. And by late night what had been a disastrous situation for the Union army has now become quite favorable. General Meade has finally arrived on the scene, as the fortification of Culp's and Cemetery hills proceeds — digging trenches, piling stones, cutting trees, and building log breastworks. Meade spends the night setting up his various corps along the great hooking stretch of hills, from Culp's Hill in the northeast, down Cemetery Ridge, to the Round Tops about three miles south. In turn, Lee spends the night assembling his army in a great enclosing ring, parallel to and wider than the Union front, some five miles in length, much of it along Seminary Ridge. Between the two ridges occupied by the two armies lies a wide band of farmland and peach orchards, the first crops of wheat and corn and grasses nearly ripe now. On either side two huge

This house behind the Gettsyburg cemetery on the road to Taneytown became General Meade's headquarters during the battle. Confederate artillery fire almost destroyed it, leaving it surrounded by dead horses.

armies prepare for a great "pitched battle," the last and largest of its kind the world will ever know.

Gettysburg is about to become immortal. The townspeople work all night. At the bank the wife of the cashier opens the bombproof vault and takes in nineteen women and children, two dogs, and a cat. All night long medical teams work on the wounded. Though the Army of the Potomac has a total of 650 doctors and 3,000 ambulance drivers and stretcher bearers, they cannot keep up with the number of wounded who lie in the fields of Cemetery Ridge. The total casualties on both sides for that first day of fighting number 17,000. All night the wounded cry in pain, dying score by score across the blood-soaked fields. Many who have not received fatal wounds will die from infections that set in almost immediately in the hot, muggy weather. For limb wounds, the routine treatment is amputation for fear of gangrene. The amputations continue day and night in the medical tents set up behind the lines of both armies.

Day two, July 2: Also a day of great losses — over sixteen thousand men are killed or wounded. The fighting is intense, much of it hand-to-hand with bayonet, as the Confederates try to pry their way onto the high ground where Meade's army has dug in. Against orders, Union Major General Daniel Sickles abandons his good position on Little Round Top and sets himself and his men below in a peach orchard. This is just the opportunity Lee is waiting for. The Confederates attack and the Federal troops back in the heights can do nothing but watch the slaughter of their fellow soldiers down below. Sickles himself will lose his right leg.

A felled Confederate sharpshooter

When the smoke clears, corpses cover the trampled wheat. Men lie among the rocks, at the foot of trees, all over the countryside, their toes in the air, their shirts split open, their stomachs already beginning to bloat in the heat. Horses lie along with the men, assuming grotesque positions as their limbs stiffen: mouths open, ears laid back for one final time. The sickening loss of human life will become known as the slaughter of the Peach Orchard, the Wheat-Field, Devil's Den.

Fighting continues. Later the Confederates have almost taken Little Round Top when Federal reinforcements make an important save. But in saving that strategic wooded knoll, Meade's line along Cemetery Ridge has been dangerously weakened in several places. Other Confederate attacks are barely repulsed. Night finally halts one particularly strong Confederate assault on Culp's Hill. By the day's end Meade has managed to hold his own along the ridges — but not by much. Nevertheless, optimism is the mood of his army. The Union position is a good one, the ammunition is holding out, and victory is expected. In addition, the day after tomorrow is the Fourth of July. A Union victory before that all-important national holiday will raise the morale of every Northerner and might even hasten the war's end.

Day three, July 3: It begins with a ferocious Confederate attack on Culp's Hill. By ten o'clock that morning, however, the assault has proved a failure. The next four hours, from ten to two, are strangely quiet. Behind the cover of Seminary Ridge, Lee is gathering his strength for an all-out attack on Cemetery Ridge, a final effort that will make use of all the rest of his artillery ammunition and that will employ fresh infantry troops just arrived from the west under Major General George Pickett.

Spirits are high over on Cemetery Ridge, where Union soldiers lie around in the grass, relaxing, waiting for orders. A large attack is expected but there is a general feeling that this ridge is defensible. A mile west, along Seminary Ridge, a different spirit pervades. Lee himself has been depressed ever since the battle's start, lacking his usual decisiveness. Lieutenant General James Longstreet is also down in the mouth, to the point of taking naps in the middle of the day. And there is reason for depression: the massive old-fashioned Confederate charge that is being contemplated looks to some as if it could turn into a monumental disaster.

Despite the prevailing depression, Lee proceeds with his plans. General Pickett is to lead nine brigades and Longstreet twice that many. The charge is to be preceded by a great bombardment aimed at destroying the Union artillery and damaging the infantry front lines.

At noon on this extremely hot day, the Union brigades assemble on Cemetery Ridge. Meade eats chicken, acquired from a nearby farmer. For two hours, a deathly, tension-filled silence reigns.

Then, at two o'clock in the afternoon, begins the largest artillery engagement of the Civil War and the largest ever on American soil. It involves approximately 250 big guns. The two sides exchange shellfire for over an hour. The noise and smoke and fire are incredible as the blasting proceeds, the powder explodes, and the Pennsylvania countryside is smothered beneath an enormous display of fireworks. Finally, the Confederate ammunition is used up. At the same time, the Union guns stop firing, and the Rebels hope that this means the Federal ammunition is also exhausted. Unknown to Lee and his staff, the Union forces have saved a supply of canister for later use — shot encasing clusters of lead slugs that spray out in widening cones, deadly within a range of 250 yards.

At three o'clock the great Confederate charge is ordered. Thousands upon thousands of men are to advance across a mile of field in block formation and then are expected to storm Cemetery Ridge and take it. Lee has entrusted Longstreet to give the order for the attack to begin but Longstreet is unable to do so in good conscience. He is so choked up that he has to delegate the job to a subordinate. Before the charge begins

Longstreet says to Pickett, "I am being crucified at the thought of the sacrifice of life this attack will make," and later, during the charge, he reemphasizes his position: "I don't want to make this attack. I would stop it now but that General Lee ordered it. I don't see how it can succeed."

And so, amid such mixed feelings, the last great old-style infantry charge in history begins. With the sun flashing off their muskets, fifteen thousand men — a phalanx of men a mile across and half a mile deep — begins to move silently, slowly, in parade fashion, out of the shadows of the trees and onto the open, sunbaked fields. Across the Emmitsburg road advances this astonishing sight. On Little Round Top, the Federals have saved a number of shells for just this occasion. They let them fly now and the Confederates are pounded on their right flank. Because of the tightness of the formation, a single shell can cut through a dozen men and leave a long rend where they fall. Heading directly at the little clump of trees below Cemetery Ridge, with George Pickett and his men in the lead, this antique military creature, a giant throw-back to how men fought in the Middle Ages, has just made it to within two hundred yards of the Union guns when the Federals open up with canister. What ensues, as the Confederates continue their ominous march, is unbelievable carnage.

A torrent of dust and smoke and human parts, veils of blood, hailstorms of bone and hunks of flesh, hands, fingers, cheeks, and bits of clothing all rise together in a hazy death-cloud over the oncoming Confederates. Hundreds fall. Still the Confederates keep advancing, closing ranks as the dead and wounded fall behind. By the time the men have finally reached the foot of Cemetery Ridge, there are so many dead and dying that no assault by the survivors can possibly take the heights. Yet only now does the real fighting begin: close-range musket-firing, bayonet thrusts, and face-to-face clubbing with musket butts. Men grunt and wheeze and snort and grimace and spit as they desperately go after one another to the finish.

And then, suddenly, the charge collapses. The surviving Confederates — less than half the number who started — turn and begin to run wildly. Pickett's charge has failed.

And Lee, too, has finally failed. It is his worst-fought battle of the war. Now all that is left is to withdraw, head home, and hope that the Yankees will not strike a deathblow on the way. On July 4, a huge wagon train, seventeen miles in length, begins the trip south toward the Potomac, aiming for a crossing point at Williamsport, Maryland. All the wounded who can survive travel have been collected. Through the day it pours rain, the sky finally opening up after three murderously hot days of battle. The great train of wagons and ambulances and staggering men heads south through the heavy rains for thirty hours, reaching Williamsport late at night on July 5. It is a ribbon of agony and despair; men cry out to be left to die in the rain by the road. The swollen river cannot be crossed for another week, but Meade does not follow up his advantage. During the night of July 13, after constructing a huge bridge across the ebbing waters of the Potomac, the tattered Confederates make their crossing.

Behind them, back in Pennsylvania, the mangled woods, the blood-soaked fields, the shattered fences, the nightmare fighting, the hallowed dead have started to become parts of a new American legend.

And now, just a few months later, Lincoln is about to insure that the brave men who died here will never be forgotten.

Here are two views of Mathew Brady observing Gettysburg battlefields soon after the fighting ended. A diligent self-promoter, Brady got most of the credit for the scenes of the Gettysburg aftermath. In truth, Alexander Gardner and Timothy O'Sullivan made most of the memorable pictures.

TWELVE

THE grand occasion certainly seemed to call for an extended parade, but after only fifteen minutes of marching the leaders had already reached their destination. The enormous crowd that had gathered on the grounds of the new cemetery now parted to let the procession through. What a din of slapped saddle leather and stomping hooves and whinnying and clapping and calling arose from the stragglers who were still snaking up the hill, only to find there was no room left for them.

The object of attention at the center of the crush was the speakers' platform. Speedily hammered together for the occasion, the platform stood three feet above the level of the ground and measured, some researchers say, a preposterously small twelve by twenty feet. No matter what the dimensions of the little stage, the chairs it supported obviously could not accommodate the enormous number of officials and dignitaries who expected to be

On the morning of November 19 an enormous crowd gathered on the grounds of the new cemetery. Several photographers — including Mathew Brady, the Weaver brothers, probably the Tyson brothers of Gettysburg, and possibly Alexander Gardner — were present that day, but no one can be sure who took which pictures. Identification of photographer is made even more difficult by the fact that Brady often bought negatives from others and put his name on them.

honored with a seat. Marshal Lamon and his men had their hands full.

The President arrived, bridled his bay to a halt, and dismounted just as the press of horse and humanity seemed most intense. As he was spotted, first by a group here, then by another there, cheer after cheer went up. Already Lamon and his host of marshals were steering the notables toward the platform. Off to the left of the crowd, the military began to assemble, while the ladies did so in a space especially reserved for them, to the right. The rest of the civilian part of the procession was given the best view of things to come; their position was dead in front. On the platform and close by there were special accommodations for the press; its members had to be within close hearing range. Newspapers represented included the *Washington Chronicle*, the *Philadelphia Press*, the *Chicago Tribune*, the *Cincinnati Gazette*, the *New York World*, the *Hanover Spectator*, the *Columbus State Journal*, and John Forney's *War Press*.

Here was Lincoln making his way slowly between two lines of waiting soldiers. Everyone wanted to meet him and say a word or two. Those who knew him already were proudly introducing him to those who didn't. Over and over again that long, thin hand was pumped, until Lincoln finally reached the platform and was able to climb its three steps. Raised above the mass now, he was all at once visible to thousands. Every hat suddenly came off for three hundred feet around. A hush followed.

Lincoln waved and waved again before he was collared by two eminent Ohioans, lame-duck Governor David Tod and the state's governor-elect, John Brough. Having shaken hands down below with a former Ohio governor, William Dennison, only a few moments before, Lincoln could not keep himself from making light of this triple pre-eminence. "Why, I have just seen Governor Dennison of Ohio," he told Tod and Brough. "How many more governors has Ohio?"

Now Chief Marshal Lamon was guiding Lincoln toward a settee

that had been placed in the center of the platform — one that decidedly had seen better days. Worn and scruffy though it was, the cushionless settee this day would support the honored royalty of the occasion: the President, at its center, flanked by Secretary Seward on his left and Mr. Everett on his right.

No one seemed to want to sit down. Everyone on the platform shuffled and milled, and a few at the sides had to do a balancing act to keep from toppling off. For along with Lincoln and Seward and Usher and Blair and Cameron, the little platform supported this day more than had been reckoned for. There was William Saunders, the cemetery's architect. There was the fiery John Forney, as well as the famous newsmen John Russell Young and Benjamin Perley Poore. There was the Reverend Doctor Henry Baugher, president of Gettysburg College, with his balding head and hooked Roman nose, as well as the Reverend T. H. Stockton, the white-thatched Senate chaplain. Participating governors also had been given special seats: Arthur Boreman of West Virginia; Augustus Bradford of Maryland; Abner Coburn of Maine; Andrew Curtin of Pennsylvania; David Tod of Ohio; Oliver Perry Morton of Indiana; Joel Parker of New Jersey; Horatio Seymour of New York. David Wills and his distinguished commissioners were of course placed in seats of honor, as were the generals and other high-ranking military officers. Elsewhere on the stand, watching over the entire group, stood Chief Marshal Lamon and his top assistant, Benjamin B. French. Fifteen or twenty additional guests, ranging from the chairman of the Republican Central Committee to Everett's daughter and son-in-law, were also jammed into the bulge on the platform. Two sisters, Sarah and Elenora Cook, sat on the steps leading up to the stand, while an eight-year-old boy named Peters swang his red-topped boots over the platform edge nearby.

With the stage packed to overflowing, the crowd stood on tiptoe, expectant; now only one element was lacking before the proceedings could start: the principal speaker, Edward Everett. Right now no one knew where he was. Mr. Wills himself had driven him to the scene in his carriage way before the parade had even begun. Was it possible that the old man, along with his official guide for the trip, Professor Michael Jacobs of Gettysburg College, could have returned to the battlefields for some last-minute observations and let the time slip past?

No, Everett was here on the site when Lincoln arrived; he just had not made his appearance yet. At sixty-nine, the grand old orator was having his usual embarrassing difficulties with his kidneys and had withdrawn to the tent he had requested be pitched adjacent to the speakers' stand. In its privacy he planned not only to relieve himself but also to rehearse parts of his speech one last time. Although Everett had specifically asked that the interior of the tent be separated into two sections — one to be used as a private toilet, the other for silent contemplation — the sectioning had not been done; and it had taken the eight or ten men and women who had accompanied him into his retreat much too long to realize the problem and scurry away so that he could be alone.

The whole trip to Gettysburg had affected Everett so much that his daughter Charlie wished she had come along the entire time to take care of him. E.E. — his name for himself — was not the miracle of youthful old age the world believed. The family had kept it a secret, but a year before, in his sixty-eighth year, he had suffered a stroke; and though the effects were gone, he was plagued now with this painful kidney condition. It would not be easy for him to play his part; he could never leave the platform before the ceremonies were over — he would be too conspicuous to have a hope of slipping away until the last amen of the last prayer was said. Charlie could not help worrying, but Lincoln had promised her that no matter how packed the crowd, he would find her a seat on the platform near her father. Charlie knew that however in control of things E.E. seemed, he was worried and frightened; the newspapers might say when all was over that he had been like a block of ice. They had done it before, and he was sensitive to criticism; he often said he wished he could be more "pachydermatous." Charlie also knew that he was exhausted. After six weeks of preparing his lengthy address and learning it by heart, her father had gone to Gettysburg two days early to drive over the battlefields and make sure everything he was going to say was exactly correct. The sights that met his sensitive old eyes were not calculated to steady the nerves. Now Charlie Wise looked at the President, who was sitting so stoically calm on the scene of such great loss of life, and she remembered attending his child Willie's funeral at the White House and watching the President's eyes fill with tears as he sobbed

The tent erected for Edward Everett's private use is visible at the right in this view taken during the ceremonies from the fringe of the crowd.

audibly through the service. If Lincoln could lose control of himself in an emotional situation, how much more easily could her father!

For over half a century Edward Everett had been an important part of the American scene. Born in 1794, he had entered Harvard at age thirteen and, although the youngest of forty-nine students, had been graduated first in his class four years later. At nineteen he was appointed pastor of Boston's prestigious and fashionable Brattle Street Church, a position he vacated after a few years in order to accept a newly established chair of Greek literature at Harvard that allowed for foreign travel and study. Politics beckoned and soon Everett was serving his state as a representative in Congress, after which he was elected governor of Massachusetts. In succession he was appointed U.S. minister to England, president of Harvard, and then secretary of state under President Millard Fillmore. He also served as U.S. senator from Massachusetts, but the hurried, hurly-burly world of politics did not really suit the refined, old-school, thin-skinned, kindly, finicky intellectual who shied from a fight and was easily hurt by criticism. Everett was growing old when he finally left Washington for his beloved, much quieter Massachusetts and almost by chance launched into a whole new career, the one he would be best remembered for — public oratory.

In 1856, at sixty-two, he created a monumental lecture on the character of George Washington, which he gave time and again in almost every large city in the country. He helped raise $70,000 to save Mount Vernon as a national landmark. Later he added a lecture on Benjamin Franklin to his repertoire. Zealously supportive of his country, elaborate in style, wordy, ornate, sentimental, but extremely precise in his use of words and historical analogy, Everett had an unexcelled reputation as a speaker and a patriot. The studious patrician with the fluid tongue misguidedly agreed to reenter the political arena in 1860 as the running mate of presidential candidate John Bell of Tennessee; their Constitutional Union party, a group of old-line conservatives, stood for doing

Edward Everett,
principal speaker
of the day

absolutely nothing about the issue of slavery. It was the election that Lincoln won with 180 electoral votes, leaving Bell and Everett far behind with 39.

Before Lincoln assumed office, Everett had never met the prairie lawyer face to face, but as the new President-elect began to be quoted in the newspapers, the elder statesman from Massachusetts commented in his private journal. "Three speeches thus far," Everett wrote, "have been of the most ordinary kind, destitute of everything, not merely of felicity and grace, but of common pertinence. He is evidently a person of very inferior cast of character, wholly unequal to the crisis."

Even after Lincoln's inauguration Everett was still an unsympathetic critic, although he did admit to the insoluble situation now facing the man from Illinois. "The last arrivals from Europe bring the comments of the English press on the President's inaugural," Everett wrote. "It is almost universally spoken of as feeble, equivocal and temporizing. . . . The truth is the President's situation is impossible."

A month after the inauguration, Everett and Lincoln finally met. "To church at St. John's," Everett commented. "The President and Mr. Seward were present. After the service I met them on the portico and Mr. Seward introduced me to the President. His manner and appearance were better than I expected them, and particularly courteous to me."

Lincoln must have been enormously curious about the aging Bostonian who had served his country in so many capacities before becoming a legendary orator, but when finally confronted by the real thing, he soon became less than impressed. At one point the Lincoln administration asked Everett if he would go to England and France as a private citizen to counteract the influence of the secessionists there. Everett insisted that if he took on the assignment, Lincoln himself would have to write him a letter making his journey official. Everett hoped to be Lincoln's special, personal ambassador, but the President flatly stated in the letter he wrote that "he bears no mission from this government." Angry and hurt, Everett decided the trip really wasn't worth the trouble. Maybe Lincoln had somehow spotted the queer strain of violence Everett had held so tightly in leash all his life, a trait that almost no one knew existed yet always created an inner turmoil on occasions of stress. Outwardly Everett managed to give an appearance of calmness and serenity. Inwardly he seethed. In any case, it would only be a year and two months after the gathering at Gettysburg that Everett's kidney trouble would flare again and a second stroke would cause his death. "His life was a truly great one," Lincoln would later write in kindness. But still, upon hearing the news of Everett's death, Lincoln privately wondered just where that greatness resided. The President didn't even seriously consider attending Everett's funeral.

※◦◎〓〓〓◎◦※

It was during the first year of the nation's civil conflict that Everett launched into a new speech he called *The Causes and Conduct of the War*. If earlier he had not been considered the top orator of his day, now he certainly took the title. On sixty different occasions all across the North, dignified old E.E. eloquently stated his war position: that the Constitution gave no states the right to secede, that the war was a war of aggression on the part of the South, that above all else the Union must be preserved. Although he would never admit it, Everett had been listening to President Lincoln most carefully.

"Rise, loyal millions of the country," Everett always started his rousing conclusion. "Hasten to the defense of the menaced Union. Come, old men and children! Come young men and maidens! . . . Come with your strong hands, come with your cunning hands: come with your swords, come with your knitting needles; come with your purses, your voices, your pens, your types, your prayers: — come one, come all, to the rescue of the country."

By the summer of 1863, there was no question about whom the newly formed commission for the establishment of a national cemetery at Gettysburg would pick as the keynote speaker. The choice had been unanimous.

But now the crowd on the hillside was growing restless; they had already waited more than an hour for the procession and Lincoln to arrive, and now another twenty minutes had passed while Everett readied himself. Charging back and forth between the rows of dignitaries on the platform was a greatly perturbed chief marshal, his high black hat askew and his usual Southern gentleman's easygoing manner considerably ruffled. Finally Everett emerged from his tent and was escorted to the platform by four governors as everybody breathed a sigh of relief. With Lamon clearing the way, Wills led the speaker past Secretary Usher, past Governor Curtin and his young son, past Benjamin B. French — all hatless once more, this time in deference to Everett's arrival — and showed the orator to the honored seat Nicolay had been saving for him beside the President. E.E. looked old and shaken. He was trembling slightly, perhaps frightened his mind would suddenly go blank at some crucial point in his speech. But at last he was finally there, in place. The long-awaited ceremonies could begin.

Filed under the heading "Crowd of citizens, soldiers etc." among the Brady negatives that reside in the National Archives in Washington, D.C., this historic picture was finally identified for what it really is in 1952. The large crowd and the marshals on horseback wearing sashes and high hats signaled Josephine Cobb, then specialist in photography at the National Archives, that the picture had to be of an important oc-

casion. By photographically enlarging a section of the broken eight-by-ten-inch glass negative — a portion about an inch wide, showing the cluster of people just to the right of the short flag that protrudes from the crowd at the far left of the picture — Miss Cobb brought to light the figures and faces on the following two pages. Extraordinarily, among them is Abraham Lincoln. (National Archives)

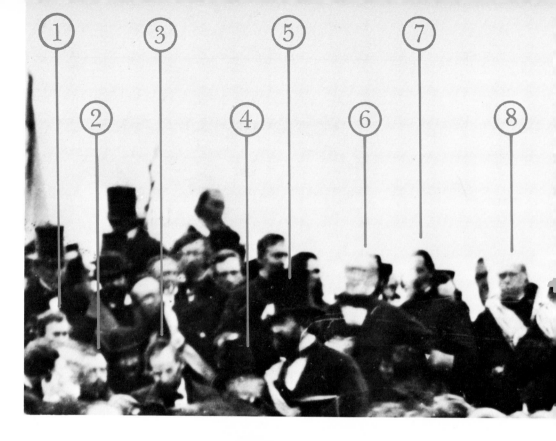

This is an enlargement of a small portion of the picture on the previous two pages. Amid the sea of indistinguishable spectators and participants, Abraham Lincoln (number 3) is now visible. This is the only known photograph of the President on the occasion of the Gettysburg Address. Because of the loss of detail caused by the extreme enlargement and by the movement of many of the people, and because it is not known exactly when during the proceedings the picture was taken, many of the identifications can never be positive. Now, however, twenty years after her original discovery, Josephine Cobb is still certain that the figure marked number 3 is Lincoln. She also believes that number 10 is Andrew Curtin, governor of Pennsylvania. Since Curtin's twelve-year-old son is known to have accompanied his father, Miss Cobb supposes that the boy marked number 9 is the Curtin youth. She thinks that number 11 is Secretary of the Interior John P. Usher. Beyond these identifications she will not venture. But other scholars will. Some are convinced that number 1 is John Hay and that number 2 is John Nicolay — Lincoln's private secretaries. These researchers also identify the figure at Lincoln's left shoulder, turning sideways, as Secretary of State William Seward (number 4).

One expert, no longer living, was convinced that the picture was taken at the moment Edward Everett, the featured orator, was finally being led onto the speakers' stand. She identified number 5 as bewhiskered Ward Hill Lamon, the chief marshal, shown leading number 6, Everett, to his seat on the settee beside Lincoln. In her

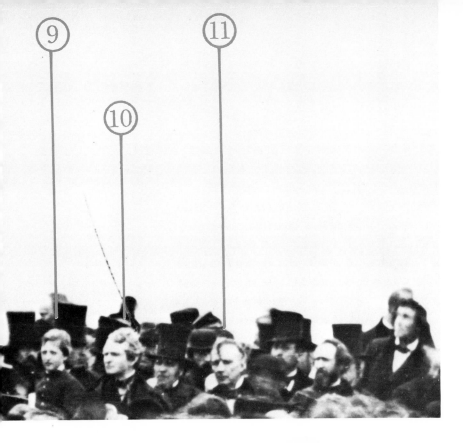

calculations number 7 is Gettysburg attorney David Wills, in charge of organizing the commemoration, and number 8 is Lamon's chief aide, Benjamin B. French. Miss Cobb disagrees about the moment the picture was taken, and therefore with the identification of Edward Everett. After studying the full picture with a magnifying glass, she concluded that many of the marshals visible in the negative are still on horseback, which indicates that the procession was still under way when the photograph was exposed. Since Everett did not make his entrance until well after the finish of the procession, Miss Cobb reasoned, he could not have been in the picture. She thinks it is more likely that number 6 is T. H. Stockton, the Senate chaplain, who delivered the invocation.

But other evidence suggests that number 6 could very well be Everett. Journalists present reported that at Everett's appearance hats were removed as a sign of respect (they had also come off for Lincoln when he arrived). A study of the picture shows that many hats are off. Even though the order of the day was no horses or wagons in the ceremony area, this ban probably did not apply to the marshals who had to keep the huge, pressing crowd in order. (At least one contemporary account substantiates this; it reported that at the start of the ceremony the crowd was so dense that the marshals on horseback could not move.) The identification of Lamon presents a problem, however, for it is believed that he was clean-shaven or had only a mustache at the time of the address. (National Archives)

THIRTEEN

ON a signal from Benjamin B. French, who was acting in Lamon's temporary absence, the ceremonies opened. First came a dirge played poignantly and with infinite care by Birgfeld's Band of Philadelphia, who almost hadn't made it to Gettysburg because of lack of funds. When the final note had rung over the hillside, the Reverend Mr. Stockton, chaplain of the Senate and a leading antislavery voice, rose, stood at the front of the platform for a moment of silence, and then launched into his carefully prepared, thousand-word prayer. It was an impressive opening, and the language made most of the audience realize the real power behind this day. As the venerable clergyman commenced his invocation, the immense crowd was surging to and fro, settling into place. But as soon as the clear tones of his voice were heard, the multitude hushed into profound silence. The white locks, pale face, and attenuated form of the speaker gave him the appearance of one who holds communion with the spirit land.

"Our heroes are not dead though their forms have fallen," Stockton concluded. "In their proper personality they are with Thee. And the spirit of their example is with Thee. It fills the air; it fills our hearts. And, as long as time shall last, it will hover on these skies and rest on this landscape, and the pilgrims of our own land and of all lands, will thrill with its inspiration, and increase, and confirm their devotion to liberty, religion, and God."

The Lord's Prayer followed, and the memories it stirred, coupled with Stockton's inspiring words, brought tears to many — Everett and Lincoln included. Over on the side of the platform, the proceedings thus far did not have a similar effect on either John Hay or Wayne MacVeagh. Hay, his eyes atwinkle, his mouth ringed with mirth, thought the prayer had gone on a bit long and whispered sardonically to MacVeagh that they had just heard "the finest invocation ever addressed to an American audience." Hay was later to elaborate on his playful observation: "Mr. Stockton made a prayer which thought it was an oration."

Now there was a reading of messages of regret from illustrious people who had been invited but could not attend. Ears pricked up when General Meade's name was called; cabinet members and congressmen were not all that important on this day, but a note from the general who had masterminded the great victory on these grounds was surely worthy of attention. Or so everyone assumed.

"It seems almost unnecessary for me to say," Meade had written, "that none can have a deeper interest in your good work than the comrades in arms, bound in close ties of long association and mutual confidence and support with those to whom you are paying this last tribute of respect. . . ." On and on Meade's message seemed to go, and its wordiness soon made the audience lose interest. (Actually, on the day of the ceremonies, Meade was headquartered in Virginia, where members

Commissioner of Public Buildings Benjamin B. French, who at last initiated the delayed ceremony. Tradition has it that he also introduced Edward Everett to the crowd, but French, Chief Marshal Lamon's right-hand man at the ceremonies, said it wasn't so. Because Longfellow and other prominent poets had declined, French wrote the dirge that was performed at Gettysburg just before Lincoln was introduced.

of his staff were entertaining four visiting Britons, including a son of the great English statesman Sir Robert Peel.)

Over on the presidential couch, Mr. Everett had spotted something he didn't like at all. He had taken the opportunity offered by the prayers and readings of regrets to study the printed program for the day, which Chief Marshal Lamon had written and had had printed in Washington. Where was the name of Edward Everett? E.E. asked himself. There was the word *Oration* — but no name of the orator. Even more surprising to the old man was the next line: "Dedication Remarks by the President of the United States." Everett, the main speaker, was not even mentioned, yet Lincoln, who was merely going to add a few appropriate remarks, was given full billing! On his copy of the program Everett now deliberately crossed out Lamon's name.

It was precisely noon when Chief Marshal Lamon stepped forward to introduce the principal speaker. Mr. Everett rose from the sofa, turned to his left, made a deep bow toward Lincoln and said, "Mr. President."

"Mr. Everett," Lincoln mouthed in return, nodding his head graciously to the old man, who cut a striking figure in his handsome, perfectly fitted suit and high-stock collar. As the orator turned to his audience, the sun caught the slightly golden tinge in his silken white hair, evidence that it had once been red. Heavy pouches protruded from beneath his slightly nearsighted eyes, and deep creases ran from the sides of his nostrils to the ends of his lips, adding marks of age to his fair, somewhat florid, almost youthful complexion.

So many times in his long and varied and honorable life of service had Mr. Everett stood before throngs of listeners and spoken eloquent, rolling, mellifluous words at dinners, at funerals, at the erection of monuments, at anniversaries, in halls, at libraries, before societies, to mourners, at historic places, in answer to toasts. No assemblage, though, equaled this one in size or importance. At least fifteen thousand people, maybe twenty thousand, were massed there in front of him, many fenced in by a huge square of soldiers. Close by lay the graves of the men whom all had come to commemorate. The whole hillside was barren of trees; the only obstruction to a bright blue sky and the countryside that had become an unforgettable battleground was a tall flagpole implanted for the day, a huge staff now surrounded by the great crowd. Strangely, its flag was not at half-mast (government flags had been ordered lowered until noon on the nineteenth); the banner swayed smartly at the very top of the

From the outskirts of the crowd of listeners the tent that had been erected for Mr. Everett's privacy can be seen just to the right of the mound of people on the speakers' stand. The gateway off to the left is the entrance to the town cemetery. When this photograph was taken, the flag was at full-mast atop the towering pole erected for the ceremonies.

pole. As Everett stood there at this pinnacle of his career, his perfectly memorized speech about to start flowing from his practiced tongue, complete silence came over the gigantic crowd. Not even a murmur could be heard.

Everett glanced at the blue heavens; yes, he could begin as he had planned. "Standing beneath this serene sky . . ." The words started to come, and even the people far away seemed to be able to hear him; his voice carried like silver bells, many thought, and had the same ringing enchantment. Borrowing from Thucydides, Everett first would set the historical precedent for a gathering like this one; how appropriate that he called upon his great cultural and historical knowledge for his most important speech.

It was appointed by law in Athens that the obsequies of the citizens who fell in battle should be performed at the public expense, and in the most honorable manner. Their bones were carefully gathered up from the funeral pyre, where their bodies were consumed, and brought home to the city. There, for three days before their interment, they lay in state, beneath tents of honor, to receive the votive offering of friends and relatives — flowers, weapons, precious ornaments, painted vases. . . . Ten coffins of funeral cypress received the honorable deposit, one for each of the tribes of the city, and an eleventh in memory of the unrecognized, but not therefore unhonored, dead, and of those whose remains could not be recovered. On the fourth day the mournful procession was formed. . . . They moved to the place of interment in that famous Ceramicus, the most beautiful suburb of Athens. . . . There, beneath the over-arching plane trees, upon a lofty stage erected for the purpose, it was ordained by law that a funeral oration should be pronounced by some citizen of Athens, in the presence of the assembled multitude.

Everett knew just when to raise and lower his voice, just which hand movements to make to emphasize a point or give a flourish to a thought. Lincoln looked on in fascination. His own speechmaking was so different: rising to his full height, he did not use his arms at all save for heated moments when he might lift his right hand and (in law partner Billy Herndon's words) "shoot . . . out that long bony forefinger of his to dot an idea or express a thought." Slow, logical, and simple, with no theatrics — that was Lincoln's style; usually there was no movement at all, except that "he used his head a great deal, . . . throwing or jerking or moving it . . . to drive the idea home." Lincoln had heard of Edward Everett's speaking powers for so long — who hadn't? — and now he listened and watched closely to discern the basis of the elder statesman's great reputation.

The President had read Everett's speeech in Washington; E.E., after having it printed in Boston and distributed to the papers to make sure that their rendition of what he said on this all-important occasion was accurate, thoughtfully had sent a copy to the White House. But it wasn't Everett's words that intrigued Lincoln most, it was the style of the man — though Lincoln could not tell that Everett, as he spoke, omitted some lines of what he had written, that several long paragraphs got condensed right there on the stand, and that a few thoughts that occurred to the speaker on the spur of the moment were extemporaneously included as he spoke. Lincoln was no doubt especially interested in Everett's long, rambling sentences and the florid, antique language — so smooth, so sculptured, so perfect in its flowing rendition.

"And shall I, fellow-citizens," Everett now asked the throng before him,

who, after an interval of twenty-three centuries, a youthful pilgrim from a world unknown to ancient Greece, have wandered over that illustrious plain, ready to put off the shoes from my feet, as one that stands on holy ground; have gazed with respectful emotion on the mound that still protects the remains of those who rolled back the tide of Persian invasion, and rescued the land of popular liberty, of letters, and arts from the ruthless foe, stand unmoved over the graves of our dear bretheren, who but yesterday — on three of those all-important days which decide a nation's history, days on whose issues depended whether this august Republican Union, founded by some of the wisest statesmen that ever lived, cemented with the blood of some of the purest patriots that ever died, should perish or endure — rolled back the tide of an invasion, not less unprovoked, not less ruthless, than that which came to plant the dark banner of Asiatic despotism and slavery on the free soil of Greece?

Yes, all one sentence! And Everett then answered himself: "Heaven forbid!"

After justifying his being there, Everett launched into a long explanation of the war and how it came about, then went into a detailed account of the Gettysburg battle, followed by his assessment of the civil strife in Europe and his prediction about the outcome of the crisis in America. Many Southerners, Everett said, were already hoping for an end to the conflict and reunification. Down south, he added, "the weary masses of the people are yearning to see the dear old [Union] flag floating upon their Capitols."

Lincoln had heard that Everett sometimes flourished a large handkerchief and shook it in the wind when referring to the flag. (Not today.) During his speech on George Washington, the great orator kept a glass of water close at hand, sipped it just before a passage about Washington's limpid purity, and with a little wave "some of the water fell," one witness testified, "in crystal drops to the floor." Everett was also known to carry around a large pocketful of coins for one particular speech he gave, so that he might jiggle them at a certain point that called for jingling bells. (Not today!)

At one point Everett said "Lee" when he meant Meade, and from his seat Lincoln softly corrected him. But the old man's memory seemed practically perfect, and this must have impressed the President, along with Everett's clear, disciplined way of speaking. Lincoln's concentration on Everett's words was visibly broken only once during the long oration, when for a moment his mind wandered to his own speech. Then he drew out his spectacles, balanced them on the bridge of his nose, and studied for a moment the two manuscript pages he had taken from his pocket. In a minute he had found what he was looking for, made some kind of decision, then quickly folded the pages back into his coat pocket and turned his attention again to the oration of the day. Quite possibly this was the moment that Lincoln decided to add "under God" to his final sentence (. . . "that this nation shall, under God, have a new birth of freedom").

At last Everett's masterly speech — so elegant, so eloquent — was over; someone had clocked it at one hour and fifty-seven minutes. Lincoln stood now and, amid the clapping, took Everett by the hand. "I am more than grateful," he said. "I am grateful to you." Seward now shook Everett's hand too, and someone threw a blanket over the shoulders of the exhausted old man.

Many in the outer rim of spectators had wandered off during the middle of Everett's speech to inspect the battlefields and search for mementos; now they seemed to return all at once, aware that the next act was about to unfold. What they heard — those who could get close enough — was a five-stanza dirge sung by the Baltimore Glee Club, an offering composed by Benjamin B. French.

> *'Tis holy ground —*
> *This spot, where, in their graves,*
> *We place our Country's braves,*
> *Who fell in Freedom's holy cause*
> *Fighting in Liberties and Laws —*
> *Let tears abound.*

By the 1860s Everett had begun to feel his age, as this detail from a Brady portrait shows. E.E. was utterly exhausted at the end of his long speech.

This and French's other four verses might have been beneath the standards of the famous poets who had been asked to compose some verse for the day; Longfellow was too busy with the publication of his *Tales of a Wayside Inn*, and Bryant and Whittier had also refused. Still, everyone was grateful to French for his night's work earlier in the month. Of course, the one American capable of matching or complementing Lincoln this day was Walt Whitman, but it is doubtful that Everett would have consented to be on the same program with any contribution from Whitman. Everett had read *Leaves of Grass* and thought it a "compound of nonsense, mysticism, the lowest materialism and the most vulgar bestiality . . . , fit to be read in the brothel and there alone."

Now, as the last notes of French's ode faded away, Ward Hill Lamon came forward from his position at the side of the platform. This is what Lincoln had wanted so badly: to see his much-maligned friend perform the solemn, cherished, and dignified act of introducing him. This is why he had pushed for his appointment as chief marshal of the day. It would be the high point of Lamon's life; nothing in his past or future would come close to this honor. Lamon practically yelled his proud introduction:

"The President of the United States."

The gatehouse to Gettysburg's village cemetery, photographed shortly after the battle

FOURTEEN

ON the settee, Lincoln turned to his secretary of state and was heard to say to him nervously just before rising, "It is a failure they won't like it." It was two o'clock. No wind stirred. Flags hung limply. Lincoln removed his gray shawl and fitted on his wire-rimmed spectacles, pushing them up the bridge of his nose. Lamon had turned toward the President and was waiting amid a fresh burst of applause. Lincoln rose — very slowly, very steadily — stretched to his full height, and stepped to the front of the platform. The boards creaked beneath his feet. Holding the two pages of his speech in one hand, he looked out over the people, running his eyes slowly over them, giving them, as was his custom, time to be at ease, and giving himself time to be completely composed.

Not far away Lincoln could see the high gatehouse of the local cemetery. The gateway was an elaborate structure — a large, corniced brick archway with windows that opened into rooms on its sides. Throughout the battle last summer, a warning sign had remained standing near the entranceway: ALL PERSONS FOUND USING FIREARMS ON THESE GROUNDS WILL BE PROSECUTED WITH THE UTMOST RIGOR OF THE LAW. As the fighting had intensified, this very gatehouse had become a crucial center of the Federal line of defense and the Confederates had bombarded the area unmercifully. Cemetery Hill, the grave sites, and the surrounding land that was today being consecrated had all been the scene of unspeakable slaughter.

Now Lincoln's eyes left the people and fixed upon the central flagpole. This was the moment when his left hand usually made an instinctive movement up to his coat, grasping the left lapel with thumb erect. He began to speak.

Many of those present had not been able to get a look at the President before now. He had been so low on the sofa, so lost in the throng of dignitaries — just another stovepipe hat and black suit in the sea of movement on the platform. All at once there was a good deal of jostling for position, amid cries of "Down in front!" and "Quiet, please!" The ensuing silence stretched back only a few hundred feet from the stand; nothing could be done about the muffled din on the outskirts, where multitudes couldn't hear a single thing Lincoln said. Making listening even more difficult, many in the crowd were preoccupied, engrossed in the actions of a photographer directly in front of the stand, who was bobbing beneath a large black cloth in an attempt to get the speaker in focus. Before the people settled down and really began to listen, the President was practically halfway through his address.

An outdoor speaker all his life, Lincoln had a high-pitched, raspy treble voice that carried out over the crowd like a bugle. He spoke slowly, deliberately, emphasizing the important words in each sentence with a marked inflection. Today Lincoln referred to his written pages only once, bringing them up close to his face and then dropping them to arm's length again. He almost never moved his feet or made any kind of gesture with his hands. In the beginning his expression was set — serious and sad — as if his mouth needed oiling, but a few sentences into the speech, the face came alive. His voice, which could be so shrill, almost squeaky at the start of a speech, would lower in tone once he got under way, losing its piping quality, turning melodious, almost musical.

The language of Lincoln's address was part and parcel of the man; he had used these words all his adult life. One part had sparks of Pericles' funeral oration in it, another of Weems's *Washington*, one of Euclid, still another of his own eulogy of Henry Clay — but most of all, the language of the address flared with sounds and images from the Scriptures. Here was his inclination, during his presidency, to couple words, a style of repetition straight out of the Prayer Book. "To *confess* and *deplore*" was a good example (italics added). "To pray with all *fervency* and *contrition*" . . . "remembrance of our own *faults* and *crimes*" . . . "by the *labors* and *sufferings* of our fathers." In his recent establishment of a Thanksgiving Day, Lincoln had used the same technique: "to *set apart* and *observe*" . . . "a day of *Thanksgiving* and *Praise*." Today he echoed the style and strength of the Prayer Book again: "*so conceived* and *so dedicated*"; "*fitting* and *proper*"; "*little note* nor *long remember*." In addition to such pairing of words, Lincoln was creating rhythm and emphasis by the lawyer's device of repeating certain words, sometimes over and over again — *dedicate, conceive, consecrate, nation, lives, living*.

As he delivered his remarks, Lincoln made a few small, apparently unintentional changes in the text he had written out, and one intentional one: the addition of "under God." Once — as he spoke the words "the world will very little note nor long remember," his lips trembled, his voice almost broke, but then it was back strong and clear again. The people strained to hear.

While the President spoke, Chief Marshal Lamon scanned the crowd, searching for danger. Back behind the press of serious listeners, a photograph was taken that would show young boys strolling with their hands in their pockets or clasped behind their backs to make them feel older for the day. Here and there on the outskirts of the crowd, little tables had been set up by local entrepreneurs who were selling not only cakes and cookies and lemonade, but battlefield relics, too — bullets and buttons and canteens and knapsacks and even cannonballs, along with wildflowers plucked from the battlefields and now displayed beneath the glass of daguerreotype cases. From a distance the speakers' stand looked like a little rise in the dark ocean of hats and heads, a small bump whence a shrill voice emanated. At a distance of several hundred feet from that voice, military rifles stacked against each other like the ribs of teepees stood every few feet in a giant ring that encircled the entire stand, each

Another view of the scene on November 19, showing stacks of muskets with bayonets in place

rifle stack attended by a soldier. The voice continued and the people stood on tiptoe, craned their necks, shaded their eyes to get a better look at the voice's origin.

What they saw first was the height of the figure, the storklike legs almost a foot longer than the trunk. When his thoughts called for it, Lincoln stretched up even beyond his normal height with an elasticity that came naturally and that he had come to use for effect. A fellow lawyer once contrasted Lincoln to another great speaker, his adversary Stephen Douglas, whom he towered over by an even foot. "While Douglas could make a powerful impression at close range, he could not reach, with both physical influence and voice, the outskirts of a mass of five or ten thousand listeners, with his short but affirmative body, as could Lincoln, with his towering form on fire with earnest and convincing words. . . . To see [Lincoln] at his best you need to be at least 10 rods in front of him, space to get the effect of his personal appearance, and time to think over what he said and how he said it."

Today Lincoln did not need to rely on his remarkable endurance; when reviewing soldiers, he could stand for two or three hours in exactly the same position. So with speaking. "Mr. Lincoln planted himself squarely on his feet at the beginning of [a] speech," a clergyman described, "with his hands clasped behind him, and stood so motionless when he spoke that a silver dollar could have been laid on the platform between his feet at the beginning and Lincoln did not move enough during his continuance to touch it with either foot."

Those lucky enough to be up close to Lincoln this day could see the face that his colleague Billy Herndon wrote about: "eyebrows cropped out like a huge jutting rock out of the brow of a hill; . . . his forehead . . . narrow, but high; his hair . . . dark, almost black, . . . floating where his fingers put it or the wind left it, piled up and tossed about like random; his cheekbones . . . high, steep and prominent . . . his jaws . . . long, upward and massive."

But people in the crowd at Gettysburg on November 19, 1863, saw Lincoln in different ways — and not quite as they pictured him from his photographs. Thirty-one known photographers took Lincoln's picture during his life, and while each caught something different, not one caught the whole man. In his 39 beardless photographs, in the 79 taken after his election as President that show him with his whiskers, in the 22 pictures taken outdoors, and in the single portrait showing him wearing his spectacles, Lincoln was never a happy-looking person. His swift aging had something to do with it. His changing hair length, its state of disorder, his growing and receding beard — all added to his many stern faces. The sternness also stemmed from the fact that when a photog-

LEFT & OPPOSITE: *The two sides of Lincoln's face, both by Brady. The picture on the right was taken in 1862, the one on the left two years later.*

rapher or artist posed Lincoln, he automatically relapsed into his sad or severe or melancholy mood, never allowing his face to react as it did when he was moved or amused or interested by something. "Graphic art was powerless," wrote Nicolay, "before a face that moved through a thousand delicate gradations of line and contour, light and shade, sparkle of the eye and curve of the lip, in the long gamut of expression from grave to gay, and back again." For finally, it was what was inside the man that made the exterior so elusive. As Herndon said, "when those little gray eyes and face were lighted up by the inward soul . . . , then it was that all those apparently ugly or homely features sprung into organs of beauty."

And all of a sudden Lincoln was done. His words had taken two minutes to say, Everett estimated. Another in the crowd said he clocked the address at exactly two minutes and fifteen seconds. Thirty-two-year-old Charles Hale — nephew of Edward Everett, younger brother of Edward Everett Hale, and an accomplished newsman — was present as one of three official members of the Massachusetts commission appointed by Governor John A. Andrew to represent the Bay State at the Pennsylvania ceremonies. Hale carefully had taken down in shorthand every word Lincoln said, using paragraphing, punctuation, and italics to indicate the President's pauses, inflection, and emphases. Hale's version is the closest we have to what Lincoln actually said that day.

Four score and seven years ago, our fathers brought forth upon this continent a new nation, conceived in liberty and dedicated to the proposition that all men are created equal.

Now we are engaged in a great civil war, testing whether that nation — or any nation, so conceived and so dedicated — can long endure.

We are met on a great battle-field of that war. We are met to dedicate a portion of it as the final resting-place of those who have given their lives that that nation might live.

It is altogether fitting and proper that we should do this.

But, in a larger sense, we cannot dedicate, we cannot consecrate, we cannot hallow, this ground. The brave men, living and dead, who struggled here, have consecrated it, far above our power to add or to detract.

The world will very little note nor long remember what we say here; but it can never forget what they did here.

It is for us, the living, rather, *to be dedicated*, here, to the unfinished work that they have thus far so nobly carried on. It is rather for us to be here dedicated to the great task remaining before us; that from these honored dead we take increased devotion to that cause for which they here gave the last full measure of devotion; that we here highly resolve that these dead shall not have died in vain; that the nation shall, under God, have a new birth of freedom, and that government of the people, by the people, for the people, shall not perish from the earth.

A working reporter and adept shorthand expert, Joseph Gilbert of the Associated Press had covered most of Lincoln's presidential speeches and thought him the easiest of any politician to follow and record because of the clarity of his voice. Today he too had taken most of the speech down, but somewhere in the middle, he claimed, he became fascinated by Lincoln's "intense earnestness and depth of feeling and I unconsciously stopped taking notes and looked up at him." After the address, Gilbert asked the President for the written manuscript, and from Lincoln's two pages he filled in and corrected his own. Gilbert's version had five minor differences in wording from Hale's, plus one word — *government* — capitalized and made plural. When asked much later about the scattering of the notation "[Applause.]" throughout his version of the address, Gilbert conceded that he had actually heard no clapping, either because of his intense concentration or because there was none. Gilbert admitted that he had indicated the applause afterward, inserting his notations wherever he thought they should go. W. H. Cunningham, another newspaperman who was near the speaker, remembered that during the address there was perfect silence. "Not a word, not a cheer, not a shout." He was positive.

Now — to a burst of applause, some accounts would say — Lincoln returned to his seat. It was reported, too, that dead silence greeted him. Afterward no one could quite remember. In any case, most of the people were stunned, bewildered. They had expected something more. And this speech, whatever its length, had been so lofty, so prayerlike; it seemed almost inappropriate to clap. The crowd had gathered at ten o'clock and now it was after two; everyone was exhausted. And somehow something was lacking. What the people had heard from their President was just too plain, too simple, too self-evident.

Joseph Becker, special artist for Frank Leslie's Illustrated Newspaper, *made this sketch on the day of the ceremonies. It was published in the December 5 issue of the popular weekly.*

FIFTEEN

IT was over. Another speech had been delivered in a lifetime of speeches. Now it could be forgotten by some, remembered as a good try by others — but still it had not been quite right for the occasion, for that huge, restless crowd, especially following the interminable main address. The President's speech could be read in tomorrow's newspapers, or, in the case of the journals whose correspondents could not get telegraph lines out of Gettysburg soon enough, in the next day's editions. The speech could be read, quickly noted, put aside and forgotten as the war continued, as life went on.

Or could it? No, this speech could not be dismissed all that quickly and easily. The strange chemistry that alters events after they have happened, making them less or more important than they had seemed at the time they occurred, was already at work. Lincoln's words had already begun to seep into the American fabric. A few spectators who had been on the scene and listened to Lincoln's remarks this day were already turning them over in their minds, considering the themes they presented, trying to remember the sequences of the words, a few of the phrases, some of their special ring and cadence.

* * *

Lincoln had taken his seat, the talk around him had ceased, and now a final dirge was sung; Dr. Baugher, the college president, pronounced the benediction and the program was over. Along with the other dignitaries, Lincoln was escorted back into town; at three o'clock he arrived at the Willses' house, where a large reception took place. First luncheon, then handshaking — lots of it — was once more in order for the President. "He received all who chose to call on him," Benjamin French wrote in his diary, "and there were thousands that took him by the hand." Whatever deep regrets Lincoln had about the outcome of his speech, he hid them well, but at the same time he brushed aside any well-meaning compliments.

Gettysburg had a local hero from the days last summer when the battle raged — its cobbler. Old John Burns had picked up his long squirrel gun and joined the Union troops, bringing down Rebel after Rebel with his deadly hunter's aim. A bullet wound in the arm finally made it impossible for him to sight, and when two more bullets struck him in the side, one glancing off his belt buckle and still another paralyzing his left leg, the most recent volunteer, seeing a Rebel charge advancing toward him, heaved aside the old squirrel rifle, buried his cartridges in the dirt, and lay as though lifeless on the ground all through the night. Left for dead, Burns was finally spotted stirring the next morning and was rescued.

Notified that Lincoln had asked to meet him, Burns arrived at the Wills house in the exact same clothes he had fought in — bullet holes and all. Later in the afternoon, the two walked arm in arm to the Pres-

OPPOSITE: *Hero John Burns was photographed at his house in Gettysburg (top photo) by Timothy O'Sullivan, and later in New York, with a multilens camera at Brady's.*

byterian Church and sat side by side in the second pew listening to a violent talk by Ohio Lieutenant Governor–elect Charles Anderson, brother of Fort Sumter's commander and hero, Robert Anderson. The speaker was as bitter toward traitors and villain-conspirators as Lincoln was forgiving, and the President listened with serious face. Before the meeting was over, Lincoln had to leave for the train, and the speech came to a temporary halt as handshakes were exchanged all the way down the aisle.

That evening all trains out of Gettysburg were held up until the President's had pulled out at six-thirty. Lincoln had an uncomfortable trip home, stretched out on the seats of chairs placed next to each other to create a crude bed. His head ached badly. Those who attended him kept a cold, wet towel on his forehead, not suspecting that the pain they were trying to soothe was the onset of a case of smallpox that, although mild, would lay the President low for the next two weeks and keep him in quarantine in the White House. Lincoln's attitude was typical: "Now I have something I can give everybody."

On the trip home passengers were discouraged from visiting the partitioned section of the rear car; but knowing that Wayne MacVeagh had to leave the train at Hanover Junction to make an appointment in Philadelphia the next day, and realizing that they had not finished yesterday's conversation on the train, Lincoln asked that the young district attorney from Pennsylvania join him. MacVeagh had been practically the only one who had congratulated Lincoln after his speech. "You did not like what I said this afternoon about your address," MacVeagh now told him, "and I have thought it over carefully and I can only say that the words you spoke will live in the land's language."

Thinking MacVeagh was merely showing kindness to a weary President who was feeling ill, Lincoln replied: "You are the only person who has such a misconception of what I said."

Not quite. Others with similar misconceptions began to be heard from. First Edward Everett. The morning following the Gettysburg ceremonies, a letter was delivered to the White House. "I should be glad," E.E. had written, "if I could flatter myself that I came as near to the central idea of the occasion, in two hours, as you did in two minutes." Robert Lincoln later remembered that Everett's letter gave his father great pleasure. The President's return letter was equally courteous, and it showed that already he had begun to change his mind on the merits of what he had said. "In our respective parts yesterday," Lincoln replied, "you could not have been excused to make a short address, nor I a long one. I am pleased to know that, in your judgment, the little I did say was not entirely a failure."

Other admirers chimed in, especially Northern newspapers sympathetic to Lincoln's presidency. "Simple and felicitous," one paper called the address; "brief and beautiful," judged another; "will live among the annals of the war"; "noble and pathetic and appropriate"; "large and lofty"; "an immortal English classic"; "the right thing in the right place"; "could the most elaborate and splendid oration be more beautiful, more touching, more inspiring, than those thrilling words of the President?"; "the few words of the President were from the heart to the heart." In general, few editors of that time considered Lincoln an eloquent speaker; "neither does he wield a polished pen," commented the *Boston Evening Transcript*. "But he has a way of saying the fitting thing." About the address at Gettysburg, the *Transcript* continued: "As reported by telegraph it is rough and loose. But the uncut fragment is full of jewels."

Other papers damned Lincoln, calling the speech "ignorant rudeness"; "insult . . . to the memory . . . of the dead"; "silly, flat and dishwatery"; "dull and commonplace." One editor found the address in "bad taste"; another thought it "spouted odious abolition doctrines"; still another could find nothing but "boorishness and vulgarity" in Lincoln's words. And one commentator judged the President's Gettysburg speech to be little else but "bottled tears and hermetically sealed grief."

The mixture of reaction to the ten sentences Lincoln strung together at Gettysburg would churn about for a while, the favorable side fueled by the European accolades that began to dribble in. But all in all, for the average American citizen, nothing either memorable and great or terrible and disastrous had happened at Gettysburg; the President had simply fulfilled another one of his obligations. Who could possibly predict what, over the roll of years, would happen to that routine fulfillment of duty?

Only 271 words — that was the final count in the version that would emerge as the authorized and official one (see the appendix). And 202 of them so short and simple: only one syllable to them. Common words — pronouns, prepositions, articles, conjunctions — little helpful words, Lincoln would have called them: *the*, eleven times; *that*, thirteen; *we*, ten times; *to* and *here*, eight times apiece; *a*, seven times; *and*, six; *of*, *have*, *can*, *for*, *not*, *it* coming up five; and a good sprinkling of *they*, *this*, *these*, and *is*, *are*, *so*, along with *but*, *in*, *us*, and *who*. Only seven words of four syllables, thirteen of three.

How could this be? How could such a conglomeration of primer words have been spun into a speech that would become known as one of the single greatest utterances in the English language, a hymn for all to learn by heart?

It did not happen overnight. Ingredients had to come together to make it live and grow. The war had to be fought and won. A bullet had to be fired in a theater box. A great tide of Lincoln adoration had to inundate the land. Imitative ceremonies had to be performed again and again on the Pennsylvania spot where they had first taken place. People present at the original event had to grow old and be asked to struggle with their memories and remember. Pens had to write a million words about Lincoln — a billion. The name of Lincoln had to become synonymous with the freeing of the slaves — "all persons held as slaves . . . are, and henceforward shall be free. . . . And upon this act, sincerely believed to be an act of justice, . . . I invoke the considerate judgment of mankind, and the gracious favor of Almighty God."

And in order for the Gettysburg speech to live and grow, Lincoln had to become in the eyes of future generations not only the man responsible for the Emancipation Proclamation but also the imperious leader who told the nation that it had better not try to persuade him to circumvent or repeal his edict. "I repeat the declaration made a year ago that 'while I remain in my present position I shall not attempt to retract or modify the emancipation proclamation,' nor shall I return to slavery any person who is free by the terms of that proclamation, or by any of the acts of Congress. If the people should, by whatever mode or means, make it an Executive duty to re-enslave such persons, another, and not I, must be their instrument to perform it."

First the name of Lincoln had to become synonymous with moral decisions and conscience, as well. Way back, when he warned that the "house divided" speech he was planning to deliver could ruin him, he said: "If it must be that I go down because of this speech, let me go down linked to the truth." And later, as President: "At all events, I must have some consciousness of being somewhere near right. I must keep some standard of principle fixed within myself."

First, too, the name of Lincoln had to become synonymous with a largeness of the spirit and a forgivingness of the heart. For he never was involved in anger or in hate. His outlook was national — even universal — not sectional. "With malice toward none, with charity for all," he said at his second inauguration, forty-two days before his death, "with firmness in the right as God gives us to see the right, let us strive on to finish the work we are in, to bind up the nation's wounds, to care for him who shall have borne the battle, and for his widow, and his orphan — to do all which may achieve and cherish a just, and a lasting peace, among ourselves, and with all nations." He had no blame for those who fought against the North, nor did he wish any harm to befall them. He was not always sure he was right, but he tried to be, knowing that anything human changes and that men and women must fit themselves to new situations.

And Lincoln's few appropriate remarks at Gettysburg had to age, had to become part of the American past, had to turn to legend; had to be memorized by a million and then millions more schoolchildren, and recited by heart standing in front of class in short trousers or a fresh dress; had to be singled out and acclaimed whenever noble statements were being judged.

Then, and only then, did the speech take its rightful place in history.

Quite a difference from that November afternoon in 1863 when Lincoln intoned his hopeful conclusion — "that the nation shall, under God, have a new birth of freedom, and that government of the people, by the people, for the people, shall not perish from the earth" — and then turned to take his place on the settee again. As he did so, John Russell Young of the *Philadelphia Press* asked him, "Is that all?" and the President said yes, it was. Then, discouraged, he turned to his chief marshal. "That speech won't scour," he said, according to Lamon. "It is a flat failure." Lamon continued his description of the scene.

"It's not what I expected," Everett said to Seward. "I'm disappointed. What did you think, Mr. Seward?"

"He has made a failure and I am sorry of it," replied the secretary of state. "His speech is not equal to him."

"What did you think of it?" Seward asked Lamon.

"I am sorry to say," Lamon answered, "it does not affect me as one of his great speeches."

Everett turned to the Chief Executive and said some polite words to him about how his speech "would live." Lincoln dismissed him. "We shall try not to talk about my address," he said. "I failed, I failed, and that is about all that can be said about it."

APPENDIX

THE VARIANT VERSIONS OF
THE GETTYSBURG ADDRESS

Even though the world long ago agreed on what words it would learn by heart and use, there are seven different versions of the Gettysburg Address worth studying.

First of all there are the two very accurate versions taken down that day in 1863 by a pair of men well trained in shorthand: Charles Hale of the Massachusetts commission and Joseph L. Gilbert of the Associated Press.

Theirs were by no means the only records of Lincoln's speech as it was delivered. "Four score and seven years ago our Fathers established upon this continent a Government subscribed in liberty and dedicated to the fundamental principle that all mankind are created equal by a good God." So the *State Journal* of Lincoln's hometown — Springfield, Illinois — began its version.

The *Philadelphia Inquirer* had its own shorthand artist on the scene. "The World will little know and nothing remember of what we see here," went the *Inquirer*'s version, ". . . but we can not forget what these brave men did here. We owe this offering to our dead. We imbibe increased devotion to that cause for which they here gave the last full measure of devotion; we here might resolve that they shall not have died in vain."

The *Missouri Republican* didn't even bother to run a version of the speech. Instead it summed up what Lincoln said, concluding: "that the government for and of the people, born in freedom, might not perish from apathy."

Forgetting these poor renditions and others, which were probably in part garbled by faulty telegraph work, we can look at the five other versions that do deserve recognition. After the big day, back in Washington, Lincoln had in his possession at least two versions of his speech in his own handwriting; his secretaries — John Nicolay and John Hay — each received one of these. Long have there been arguments as to which of these was written first and whether one or both preceded the speech or instead were jotted down by Lincoln afterward in attempts to recreate what he had said. There will never be a definitive answer, but today the best thinking is that both were written before the speech, as drafts of what the President planned to say. No one knows how many attempts at the right wording there were before these two drafts were made, how many came after, or, in fact, if there were any drafts at all other than these. There were surely notes, for Lincoln was in the habit of jotting down ideas on strips of paper and finally piecing them together.

The draft that Hay got appears to be the earlier of the two (although it is not commonly held to be). The Hay draft, with its corrections, is very close to the speech delivered by Lincoln and reported from the scene by Charles Hale and Joseph Gilbert. It was written in pencil on two ruled sheets of paper; on them Lincoln crossed out five words and above them wrote in substitutes. He also added three words elsewhere, above little upward-pointing carets. One repeated word was also crossed out. The beginning of the speech in this draft was unrevised until the end of the eighth line, and none of the changes that followed were significant. *We are met* became *we have come* — in order, presumably, not to repeat the *we are met* in the previous sentence. A *the* became an *a;* an *of* became a *for; poor* was inserted before *power; work,* somehow omitted after *unfinished,* was inserted; an *us* was added; a *the* became a *that;* and a repetition of the word *gave* was crossed out.

In the Nicolay draft, virtually all of the changes made on the Hay version are incorporated in the text. And the Nicolay version is carefully handwritten, as if it were copied — in fact, as if it were going to be read from. The first page — written in ink on official, though undated, "Executive Mansion" stationery — was probably done in Washington. The sentence "It is altogether fitting and proper that we should do this" has been altered to read "This we may, in all propriety do." Even though Lincoln used the "fitting and proper" sentence when he delivered the address, many researchers have guessed that this Executive Mansion first page was the very one Lincoln held on the platform.

As this Executive Mansion page in the Nicolay version closes, however, garbling begins. The original last sentence on the first page does not continue on the second page, which is written entirely in pencil on foolscap and was probably a Gettysburg addition. Instead, the final words on the first page — *to stand here* — are crossed out in pencil and the phrase *we here be dedica*[*ted*] is written in at the point where the pages break, creating a confusing transition in midsentence (after *It is for us, the living*). Furthermore, the writing on the second page, in changing the original wording and jumping from the Executive Mansion page, does not carry over the complete text of the speech as it was delivered: a sentence break is dropped, along with twenty-two words between two uses of the word *dedicated*, one of which is also omitted. Lincoln probably spotted his mistake and went back to the writing table in the Willses' guest room to make a corrected second page, which he used on the platform. But somehow, what Nicolay got afterward was the finished first page and a flawed, outdated, yet undiscarded second page.

Both the Nicolay and Hay drafts eventually found their way to the Library of Congress, where they reside today.

In the months after the speech was delivered, Lincoln wrote out at least three copies of his address, all in ink, to fulfill requests. He not only had his drafts and his prodigious memory to work from, but also could consult printed versions from the newspapers and a pamphlet that had been issued by Little, Brown and Company of Boston.

The first of these after-the-fact copies by Lincoln was made at the request of Edward Everett, in behalf of New York's Metropolitan Fair, scheduled for the spring of 1864. The document was to be sold to the highest bidder, along with Everett's manuscript, to help raise money for the care of wounded soldiers. This version, which first sold for $1,000 and much later would bring $150,000, was finally acquired in 1944 for the state of Illinois (with the help of a hefty gift from Marshall Field and $60,000 in pennies from Illinois schoolchildren).

By the time Lincoln made this copy, he could not still have considered his efforts at Gettysburg a failure. The words were beginning to take on a luster; penned in his own handwriting, they were coming to be considered valuable and historic. Edward Everett's "finished text" of his own speech was in many ways quite different from what he actually said, but this did not seem to worry anyone — for back then, before electronic recordings, it was the prerogative of speakers to deliver orations and then touch up the transcriptions as they saw fit before final publication. Lincoln, therefore, had no qualms, in his subsequent copies of his Gettysburg speech, about changing an *upon* to *on*, deleting a *here*, adding a *that*, adding *who fought here*, changing *carried on* to *advanced*. In the copies he made afterward, Lincoln kept tinkering with the punctuation, too. The one change that he had made extemporaneously, as he was giving the speech — the addition of the phrase *under God* — remained as a permanent part of all three subsequent copies.

The second copy Lincoln made in his own hand after delivering the speech — a version written at the request of George Bancroft, the noted historian and statesman — was done to benefit the Maryland Soldiers' and Sailors' Fair at Baltimore. A few minor changes from the Everett version appeared on Lincoln's first try for Bancroft. But because fair officials needed a titled, dated, and signed manuscript suitable for facsimile reproduction in a projected book, this version was rejected: Lincoln had made it using two sides of a single piece of paper and had left off the trimmings. Bancroft kept it. It is now owned by Cornell University.

Lincoln made still another copy, this time using two pieces of paper and adding a heading — "Address delivered at the dedication of the Cemetery at Gettysburg" — plus a signature and date at the end ("Abraham Lincoln" at right and "November 19, 1863" at left, slightly lower than the name). Now the manuscript was in proper shape to be included in *Autograph Leaves of Our Country's Authors*, the volume to be sold by the fair. The President sent this "final" version of his speech to the Baltimore committee on March 11, 1864, almost four months after making the address. Again there were some slight changes in the wording. This copy has come to be known as the Bliss manuscript — after its subsequent owner Alexander Bliss of Baltimore. In 1949 a former Cuban ambassador to the United States bought it for $54,000. Upon his death, the manuscript went to the government of the United States, to be displayed in the White House — where it is today, hanging in the First Family's private quarters.

As the speech took on more and more prominence, questions arose as to which version should be considered official. In 1895 Congress called for a decision. With the concurrence of the President's son Robert, the last-known handwritten copy — the Bliss-Baltimore version — was chosen as Abraham Lincoln's own last word on the subject. This is the version we all learn today, the one inscribed in so many places around the nation and the world.

The accompanying illustrations are facsimilies of the five existing versions of the Gettysburg Address in Lincoln's own hand. Following them is a phrase-by-phrase textual comparison of the seven reliable existing versions of the Gettysburg Address as it was originally recorded. Number 1 is the Hay draft, followed by version 2, the draft given to Nicolay. Number 3 is Gilbert's AP report, taken down in shorthand on the scene and checked by the reporter against Lincoln's speaking notes just after the address. Number 4 is the shorthand transcription by Charles Hale, probably the most accurate rendering of the words Lincoln spoke. Versions 5, 6, and 7 are the copies written out by Lincoln in the months after the speech had been delivered: number 5 is the Everett version, 6 is the Bancroft version, and 7 is the well-known Bliss version.

Four score and seven years ago our fathers
brought forth, upon this continent, a new nation, conceived in Liberty, and dedicated to the proposition
that all men are created equal.

Now we are engaged in a great civil war, testing whether that nation, or any nation, so conceived,
and so dedicated, can long endure. We are met
here on a great battle-field of that war. We have
come
not to dedicate a portion of it as a final rest-
for
ing place of those who here gave their lives that
that nation might live. It is altogether fitting
and proper that we should do this.

But in a larger sense we can not dedicate—
we can not consecrate— we can not hallow this
ground. The brave men, living and dead, who struggled here, have consecrated it far above our poor power
to add or detract. The world will little note,
nor long remember, what we say here, but
can never forget what they did here. It is
for us, the living, rather to be dedicated
work
here to the unfinished, which they have,
thus far, so nobly carried on. It is rather

for us to be here dedicated to the great
task remaining before us — that from these
honored dead we take increased devotion
to the cause for which they here gave
the last full measure of devotion — that
we here highly resolve that these dead
shall not have died in vain; that this
nation shall have a new birth of freedom;
and that this government of the people, by
the people, for the people, shall not perish
from the earth.

Executive Mansion.

Washington,   , 186 .

Four scores and seven years ago our fathers brought
forth, upon this continent, a new nation, conceived
in liberty, and dedicated to the proposition that
"all men are created equal"

Now we are engaged in a great civil war, testing
whether that nation, or any nation so conceived,
and so dedicated, can long endure. We are met
on a great battle field of that war. We have
come to dedicate a portion of it, as a final resting place for those who died here, that the nation
might live. This we may, in all propriety do. But, in a
larger sense, we can not dedicate— we can not
consecrate— we can not hallow, this ground—
The brave men, living and dead, who struggled
here, have hallowed it, far above our poor power
to add or detract. The world will little note, nor long
remember what we say here; while it can never
forget what they did here.

It is rather for us, the living, to stand here,

2. Nicolay draft
(Library of Congress)

ted to the great task remaining before us—
that, from these honored dead we take increased devotion to that cause for which
they here, gave the last, full measure of devotion— that we here highly resolve these
dead shall not have died in vain, that
this nation, shall have a new birth of freedom, and that government. of the people by
the people for. the people, shall not perish from the earth.

5. *Everett copy*
(Illinois State
Historical Library)

Four score and seven years ago our fathers brought forth upon this continent, a new nation, conceived in Liberty, and dedicated to the proposition that all men are created equal.

Now we are engaged in a great civil war, testing whether that nation, or any nation so conceived, and so dedicated, can long endure. We are met on a great battle-field of that war. We have come to dedicate a portion of that field, as a final resting place for those who here gave their lives, that that nation might live. It is altogether fitting and proper that we should do this.

But, in a larger sense, we can not dedicate— we can not consecrate— we can not hallow— this ground. The brave men, living and dead, who struggled here, have consecrated it, far above our poor power to add or detract. The world will little note, nor long remember, what we say here, but it can never forget what they did here. It is for us, the living, rather, to be dedicated here to the unfinished work which they who fought here, have, thus far, so nobly advanced. It is rather for us to be here dedicated to the great task remaining before

us— that from these honored dead we take increas=
ed devotion to that cause for which they here gave
the last full measure of devotion— that we here
highly resolve that these dead shall not have
died in vain— that this nation, under God,
shall have a new birth of freedom— and that,
government of the people, by the people, for the
people, shall not perish from the earth.

Four score and seven years ago our fathers brought forth, on this continent, a new nation, conceived in Liberty, and dedicated to the proposition that all men are created equal.

Now we are engaged in a great civil war, testing whether that nation, or any nation so conceived, and so dedicated, can long endure. We are met on a great battle-field of that war. We have come to dedicate a portion of that field, as a final resting-place for those who here gave their lives, that that nation might live. It is altogether fitting and proper that we should do this.

But, in a larger sense, we can not dedicate— we can not consecrate— we can not hallow— this ground. The brave men, living and dead, who struggled here, have consecrated it far above our poor power to add or detract. The world will little note, nor long remember what we say here, but it can never forget what they did here. It is for us the living, rather, to be dedicated here to the unfinished work which they who fought here have thus far so nobly advanced. It is rather for us to be here dedicated to the great task remaining be-

6. *Bancroft copy*
(Cornell University)

fore us— that from these honored dead we take increased devotion to that cause for which they here gave
the last full measure of devotion— that we here highly resolve that these dead shall not have died in
vain— that this nation, under God, shall have
a new birth of freedom— and that government
of the people, by the people, for the people, shall
not perish from the earth.

7. *Bliss copy*
(Bettmann Archive)

Address delivered at the dedication of the Cemetery at Gettysburg.

Four score and seven years ago our fathers brought forth on this continent, a new nation, conceived in Liberty, and dedicated to the proposition that all men are created equal.

Now we are engaged in a great civil war, testing whether that nation, or any nation so conceived and so dedicated, can long endure. We are met on a great battle field of that war. We have come to dedicate a portion of that field, as a final resting place for those who here gave their lives that that nation might live. It is altogether fitting and proper that we should do this.

But, in a larger sense, we can not dedicate — we can not consecrate — we can not hallow — this ground. The brave men, living and dead, who struggled here have consecrated it, far above our poor power to add or detract. The world will little note, nor long remember what we say here, but it can never forget what they did here. It is for us the living, rather, to be dedicated here to the unfinished work which they who fought here have thus far so nobly advanced. It is rather for us to be here dedicated to the great task remaining before us — that from these honored dead we take increased devotion to that cause for which they gave the last full measure of devotion — that we here highly resolve that these dead shall not have died in vain — that this nation, under God, shall have a new birth of freedom — and that government of the people, by the people, for the people, shall not perish from the earth.

Abraham Lincoln.

November 19. 1863.

1. HAY DRAFT:	Four score and seven years ago
2. NICOLAY DRAFT:	Four score and seven years ago
3. GILBERT REPORT:	Four score and seven years ago
4. HALE REPORT:	Four score and seven years ago,
5. EVERETT COPY:	Four score and seven years ago
6. BANCROFT COPY:	Four score and seven years ago
7. BLISS COPY:	Four score and seven years ago

1. HAY DRAFT:	our fathers brought forth, upon this continent,
2. NICOLAY DRAFT:	our fathers brought forth, upon this continent,
3. GILBERT REPORT:	our fathers brought forth upon this continent
4. HALE REPORT:	our fathers brought forth upon this continent
5. EVERETT COPY:	our fathers brought forth upon this continent,
6. BANCROFT COPY:	our fathers brought forth, on this continent,
7. BLISS COPY:	our fathers brought forth on this continent,

1. HAY DRAFT:	a new nation, conceived in Liberty,
2. NICOLAY DRAFT:	a new nation, conceived in liberty,
3. GILBERT REPORT:	a new Nation, conceived in Liberty,
4. HALE REPORT:	a new nation, conceived in liberty
5. EVERETT COPY:	a new nation, conceived in Liberty,
6. BANCROFT COPY:	a new nation, conceived in Liberty,
7. BLISS COPY:	a new nation, conceived in Liberty,

1. HAY DRAFT: and dedicated to the proposition
2. NICOLAY DRAFT: and dedicated to the proposition
3. GILBERT REPORT: and dedicated to the proposition
4. HALE REPORT: and dedicated to the proposition
5. EVERETT COPY: and dedicated to the proposition
6. BANCROFT COPY: and dedicated to the proposition
7. BLISS COPY: and dedicated to the proposition

1. HAY DRAFT: that all men are created equal.
2. NICOLAY DRAFT: that "all men are created equal"
3. GILBERT REPORT: that all men are created equal. [Applause.]
4. HALE REPORT: that all men are created equal.
5. EVERETT COPY: that all men are created equal.
6. BANCROFT COPY: that all men are created equal.
7. BLISS COPY: that all men are created equal.

1. HAY DRAFT: Now we are engaged in a great civil war,
2. NICOLAY DRAFT: Now we are engaged in a great civil war,
3. GILBERT REPORT: Now we are engaged in a great civil war,
4. HALE REPORT: Now we are engaged in a great civil war,
5. EVERETT COPY: Now we are engaged in a great civil war,
6. BANCROFT COPY: Now we are engaged in a great civil war,
7. BLISS COPY: Now we are engaged in a great civil war;

1.	HAY DRAFT:	testing whether that nation, or any nation,
2.	NICOLAY DRAFT:	testing whether that nation, or any nation
3.	GILBERT REPORT:	testing whether that Nation or any Nation
4.	HALE REPORT:	testing whether that nation — or any nation,
5.	EVERETT COPY:	testing whether that nation, or any nation
6.	BANCROFT COPY:	testing whether that nation, or any nation
7.	BLISS COPY:	testing whether that nation, or any nation

1.	HAY DRAFT:	so conceived, and so dedicated, can long endure.
2.	NICOLAY DRAFT:	so conceived, and so dedicated, can long endure.
3.	GILBERT REPORT:	so conceived and so dedicated can long endure.
4.	HALE REPORT:	so conceived and so dedicated — can long endure.
5.	EVERETT COPY:	so conceived, and so dedicated, can long endure.
6.	BANCROFT COPY:	so conceived, and so dedicated, can long endure.
7.	BLISS COPY:	so conceived and so dedicated, can long endure.

1.	HAY DRAFT:	We are met here on a great battle-field of that war.
2.	NICOLAY DRAFT:	We are met on a great battle field of that war.
3.	GILBERT REPORT:	We are met on a great battle-field of that war.
4.	HALE REPORT:	We are met on a great battle-field of that war.
5.	EVERETT COPY:	We are met on a great battle-field of that war.
6.	BANCROFT COPY:	We are met on a great battle-field of that war.
7.	BLISS COPY:	We are met on a great battle-field of that war.

1. HAY DRAFT:	We have come to dedicate a portion of it
2. NICOLAY DRAFT:	We have come to dedicate a portion of it,
3. GILBERT REPORT:	We are met to dedicate a portion of it
4. HALE REPORT:	We are met to dedicate a portion of it
5. EVERETT COPY:	We have come to dedicate a portion of that field,
6. BANCROFT COPY:	We have come to dedicate a portion of that field,
7. BLISS COPY:	We have come to dedicate a portion of that field,

1. HAY DRAFT:	as a final resting place for those
2. NICOLAY DRAFT:	as a final resting place for those
3. GILBERT REPORT:	as the final resting-place of those
4. HALE REPORT:	as the final resting-place of those
5. EVERETT COPY:	as a final resting place for those
6. BANCROFT COPY:	as a final resting-place for those
7. BLISS COPY:	as a final resting place for those

1. HAY DRAFT:	who here gave their lives that that nation might live.
2. NICOLAY DRAFT:	who died here, that the nation might live.
3. GILBERT REPORT:	who here gave their lives that that nation might live.
4. HALE REPORT:	who have given their lives that that nation might live.
5. EVERETT COPY:	who here gave their lives, that that nation might live.
6. BANCROFT COPY:	who here gave their lives, that that nation might live.
7. BLISS COPY:	who here gave their lives that that nation might live.

1. HAY DRAFT:	It is altogether fitting
2. NICOLAY DRAFT:	This we may,
3. GILBERT REPORT:	It is altogether fitting
4. HALE REPORT:	It is altogether fitting
5. EVERETT COPY:	It is altogether fitting
6. BANCROFT COPY:	It is altogether fitting
7. BLISS COPY:	It is altogether fitting

1. HAY DRAFT:	and proper that we should do this.
2. NICOLAY DRAFT:	in all propriety do.
3. GILBERT REPORT:	and proper that we should do this.
4. HALE REPORT:	and proper that we should do this.
5. EVERETT COPY:	and proper that we should do this.
6. BANCROFT COPY:	and proper that we should do this.
7. BLISS COPY:	and proper that we should do this.

1. HAY DRAFT:	But in a larger sense we can not dedicate —
2. NICOLAY DRAFT:	But, in a larger sense, we can not dedicate —
3. GILBERT REPORT:	But in a larger sense we cannot dedicate,
4. HALE REPORT:	But, in a larger sense, we cannot dedicate,
5. EVERETT COPY:	But, in a larger sense, we can not dedicate —
6. BANCROFT COPY:	But, in a larger sense, we can not dedicate —
7. BLISS COPY:	But, in a larger sense, we can not dedicate —

1. HAY DRAFT:	we can not consecrate — we can not hallow this ground.
2. NICOLAY DRAFT:	we can not consecrate — we can not hallow, this ground —
3. GILBERT REPORT:	we cannot consecrate, we cannot hallow this ground.
4. HALE REPORT:	we cannot consecrate, we cannot hallow, this ground.
5. EVERETT COPY:	we can not consecrate — we can not hallow — this ground.
6. BANCROFT COPY:	we can not consecrate — we can not hallow — this ground.
7. BLISS COPY:	we can not consecrate — we can not hallow — this ground.

1. HAY DRAFT:	The brave men, living and dead,
2. NICOLAY DRAFT:	The brave men, living and dead,
3. GILBERT REPORT:	The brave men living and dead
4. HALE REPORT:	The brave men, living and dead,
5. EVERETT COPY:	The brave men, living and dead,
6. BANCROFT COPY:	The brave men, living and dead,
7. BLISS COPY:	The brave men, living and dead,

1. HAY DRAFT:	who struggled here, have consecrated it
2. NICOLAY DRAFT:	who struggled here, have hallowed it,
3. GILBERT REPORT:	who struggled here have consecrated it
4. HALE REPORT:	who struggled here, have consecrated it,
5. EVERETT COPY:	who struggled here, have consecrated it,
6. BANCROFT COPY:	who struggled here, have consecrated it
7. BLISS COPY:	who struggled here have consecrated it,

1.	HAY DRAFT:	far above our poor power to add or detract.
2.	NICOLAY DRAFT:	far above our poor power to add or detract.
3.	GILBERT REPORT:	far above our power to add or detract. [Applause.]
4.	HALE REPORT:	far above our power to add or to detract.
5.	EVERETT COPY:	far above our poor power to add or detract.
6.	BANCROFT COPY:	far above our poor power to add or detract.
7.	BLISS COPY:	far above our poor power to add or detract.

1.	HAY DRAFT:	The world will little note,
2.	NICOLAY DRAFT:	The world will little note,
3.	GILBERT REPORT:	The world will little note
4.	HALE REPORT:	The world will very little note
5.	EVERETT COPY:	The world will little note,
6.	BANCROFT COPY:	The world will little note,
7.	BLISS COPY:	The world will little note,

1.	HAY DRAFT:	nor long remember, what we say here,
2.	NICOLAY DRAFT:	nor long remember what we say here;
3.	GILBERT REPORT:	nor long remember what we say here,
4.	HALE REPORT:	nor long remember what we say here;
5.	EVERETT COPY:	nor long remember, what we say here,
6.	BANCROFT COPY:	nor long remember what we say here,
7.	BLISS COPY:	nor long remember what we say here,

1. HAY DRAFT:	but can never forget what they did here.
2. NICOLAY DRAFT:	while it can never forget what they *did* here.
3. GILBERT REPORT:	but it can never forget what they did here. [Applause.]
4. HALE REPORT:	but it can never forget what they did here.
5. EVERETT COPY:	but it can never forget what they did here.
6. BANCROFT COPY:	but it can never forget what they did here.
7. BLISS COPY:	but it can never forget what they did here.

1. HAY DRAFT:	It is for us, the living, rather to be dedicated here
2. NICOLAY DRAFT:	It is rather for us, the living, we here be dedicated
3. GILBERT REPORT:	It is for us, the living, rather to be dedicated here
4. HALE REPORT:	It is for us, the living, rather, *to be dedicated*, here,
5. EVERETT COPY:	It is for us, the living, rather, to be dedicated here
6. BANCROFT COPY:	It is for us the living, rather, to be dedicated here
7. BLISS COPY:	It is for us the living, rather, to be dedicated here

1. HAY DRAFT:	to the unfinished work which they have,
2. NICOLAY DRAFT:	
3. GILBERT REPORT:	to the unfinished work that they have
4. HALE REPORT:	to the unfinished work that they have
5. EVERETT COPY:	to the unfinished work which they who fought here, have,
6. BANCROFT COPY:	to the unfinished work which they who fought here have
7. BLISS COPY:	to the unfinished work which they who fought here have

1. HAY DRAFT: thus far, so nobly carried on.

2. NICOLAY DRAFT:

3. GILBERT REPORT: thus far so nobly carried on. [Applause.]

4. HALE REPORT: thus far so nobly carried on.

5. EVERETT COPY: thus far, so nobly advanced.

6. BANCROFT COPY: thus far so nobly advanced.

7. BLISS COPY: thus far so nobly advanced.

1. HAY DRAFT: It is rather for us to be here dedicated

2. NICOLAY DRAFT:

3. GILBERT REPORT: It is rather for us to be here dedicated

4. HALE REPORT: It is rather for us to be here dedicated

5. EVERETT COPY: It is rather for us to be here dedicated

6. BANCROFT COPY: It is rather for us to be here dedicated

7. BLISS COPY: It is rather for us to be here dedicated

1. HAY DRAFT: to the great task remaining before us —

2. NICOLAY DRAFT: to the great task remaining before us —

3. GILBERT REPORT: to the great task remaining before us,

4. HALE REPORT: to the great task remaining before us;

5. EVERETT COPY: to the great task remaining before us —

6. BANCROFT COPY: to the great task remaining before us —

7. BLISS COPY: to the great task remaining before us —

1. HAY DRAFT:	that from these honored dead we take increased devotion
2. NICOLAY DRAFT:	that, from these honored dead we take increased devotion
3. GILBERT REPORT:	that from these honored dead we take increased devotion
4. HALE REPORT:	that from these honored dead we take increased devotion
5. EVERETT COPY:	that from these honored dead we take increased devotion
6. BANCROFT COPY:	that from these honored dead we take increased devotion
7. BLISS COPY:	that from these honored dead we take increased devotion

1. HAY DRAFT:	to that cause for which they here gave
2. NICOLAY DRAFT:	to that cause for which they here, gave
3. GILBERT REPORT:	to that cause for which they here gave
4. HALE REPORT:	to that cause for which they here gave
5. EVERETT COPY:	to that cause for which they here gave
6. BANCROFT COPY:	to that cause for which they here gave
7. BLISS COPY:	to that cause for which they gave

1. HAY DRAFT:	the last full measure of devotion —
2. NICOLAY DRAFT:	the last full measure of devotion —
3. GILBERT REPORT:	the last full measure of devotion;
4. HALE REPORT:	the last full measure of devotion;
5. EVERETT COPY:	the last full measure of devotion —
6. BANCROFT COPY:	the last full measure of devotion —
7. BLISS COPY:	the last full measure of devotion —

1. HAY DRAFT:	that we here highly resolve that these dead
2. NICOLAY DRAFT:	that we here highly resolve these dead
3. GILBERT REPORT:	that we here highly resolve that the dead
4. HALE REPORT:	that we here highly resolve that these dead
5. EVERETT COPY:	that we here highly resolve that these dead
6. BANCROFT COPY:	that we here highly resolve that these dead
7. BLISS COPY:	that we here highly resolve that these dead

1. HAY DRAFT:	shall not have died in vain;
2. NICOLAY DRAFT:	shall not have died in vain;
3. GILBERT REPORT:	shall not have died in vain [applause];
4. HALE REPORT:	shall not have died in vain;
5. EVERETT COPY:	shall not have died in vain —
6. BANCROFT COPY:	shall not have died in vain —
7. BLISS COPY:	shall not have died in vain —

1. HAY DRAFT:	that this nation shall have
2. NICOLAY DRAFT:	that the nation, shall have
3. GILBERT REPORT:	that the nation shall, under God, have
4. HALE REPORT:	that the nation shall, under God, have
5. EVERETT COPY:	that this nation, under God, shall have
6. BANCROFT COPY:	that this nation, under God, shall have
7. BLISS COPY:	that this nation, under God, shall have

1. HAY DRAFT: a new birth of freedom; and that this government

2. NICOLAY DRAFT: a new birth of freedom, and that government

3. GILBERT REPORT: a new birth of freedom; and that Governments

4. HALE REPORT: a new birth of freedom, and that government

5. EVERETT COPY: a new birth of freedom — and that, government

6. BANCROFT COPY: a new birth of freedom — and that government

7. BLISS COPY: a new birth of freedom — and that government

1. HAY DRAFT: of the people, by the people, for the people,

2. NICOLAY DRAFT: of the people by the people for the people,

3. GILBERT REPORT: of the people, by the people, and for the people,

4. HALE REPORT: of the people, by the people, for the people,

5. EVERETT COPY: of the people, by the people, for the people,

6. BANCROFT COPY: of the people, by the people, for the people,

7. BLISS COPY: of the people, by the people, for the people,

1. HAY DRAFT: shall not perish from the earth.

2. NICOLAY DRAFT: shall not perish from the earth.

3. GILBERT REPORT: shall not perish from the earth. [Long-continued applause.]

4. HALE REPORT: shall not perish from the earth.

5. EVERETT COPY: shall not perish from the earth.

6. BANCROFT COPY: shall not perish from the earth.

7. BLISS COPY: shall not perish from the earth.

ACKNOWLEDGMENTS

I have already mentioned my debts to my grandfather and my mother. Two other members of my family loom large in the creation of this book. For six years now my wife Katharine has put up with enormous piles of moldy books and old newspapers and ancient magazines and dusty scrapbooks as our early mornings, late evenings, weekends, and vacations have been dominated by Lincoln and his speech at Gettysburg. How she has lived and sneezed her way through it all I will never know, but I lovingly thank her. I also thank my oldest son, Philip B. Kunhardt III, who has done major research for me, in particular in the areas of Lincoln's life, his writings, and the Gettysburg battle. His exhaustive notes, his intelligent and creative interpretations and analyses along the way, and his sensitive and imaginative suggestions when the first draft of the book was done were of incalculable value.

My friend Cindy Allen came up to New York one summer from North Carolina and worked in libraries and archives, painting a picture for me of what the world was like in November 1863.

Another friend, Robin Richman, helped me in Washington, doing invaluable scouting and research in our nation's archives.

Ann Morrell not only interpreted my scratches and scrawls and typed this whole book, she was also a close friend and critic throughout its creation.

Ralph Graves, editorial director of Time Inc. and the best word editor I've ever run across in my thirty-three years in the magazine and book world, volunteered to work his magic on my manuscript. My longtime associate and friend did just that.

Barbara Baker Burrows, also an old friend, helped gather the facsimiles of the address itself.

And then, of course, there is dear friend Josephine Cobb, retired now for ten years from her job as the National Archives' picture historian, who helped me immeasurably with the manuscript and photograph captions, just as she helped my mother before me and my grandfather before her.

Old friends — where would we be without them? But I also want to acknowledge some new ones. First, Ray Roberts, my editor at Little, Brown. One of the dreariest things a book editor has to face is inheriting a lot of manuscripts that someone else, now departed, initiated. In this case Ray took over a project initiated years earlier by my old friend Robert Emmett Ginna, Jr., formerly Little, Brown's editor in chief. Much to Ray's credit and to my benefit, he got caught up in the same excitement Bob had felt way back when the idea for this book filled just two pieces of paper.

Two more Little, Brown editors I must add to this list — Michael Brandon, who did the final editing, checking, styling, and smoothing with a thoroughness and zest that astounded me; and Ann Sleeper, who tended my manuscript throughout its Boston days with extraordinary care and thoughtfulness.

INDEX

Page numbers in *italics* indicate illustrations and captions.

Adams Express Company, 32
Adams Sentinel, 32
Alleman, M. J., 100–101
Allen, Major E. J. *See* Pinkerton, Allan
"all men are created equal" clause: quoted by AL, 26, 60, 214 (*and see appendix*); and Lincoln-Douglas debates, 145–146
amputation, *11*, 171–172
Anderson, Charles, 220
Anderson, Colonel Robert, 100, 220
Andrew, John A., 214
Animated Nature, 63
Antietam, *72*, 81
Ashmun, George, 152
Autograph Leaves of Our Country's Authors, 230

Baltimore, AL assassination plot in, 95
Baltimore & Ohio Railroad, 71, 85, 95
Baltimore Fire Department, 32
Baltimore Glee Club, 118, 203
Bancroft, George, 230
Bancroft copy (of Gettysburg Address), 230, *238–239*, 242–253
Bates, Edward, 85, 86
battles. *See under individual locations*
Baugher, Henry, 182, 218
Beauregard, General P. G. T., 82
Becker, Joseph, *216*
Bell, John, 185, 187
Bertinatti, Joseph, 93–94
Biesecker, F. W., 36
Bingham, Sergeant H. Paxton, *117*, 118, 121
Birgfeld's Band, 195

Black Hawk War, AL in, 133
Blair, Francis P., 89–90
Blair, Montgomery, 85, 86, *88*, 89–90, 95, 161, 182
Bliss, Alexander, 230
Bliss copy (of Gettysburg Address), 230–231, *240–241*, 242–253
books, AL and, 19, 42, 52, 61–63, 131, *135*, 142
Boone, Daniel, 126
Booth, John Wilkes, 43
Boreman, Arthur, 182
Boston Daily Advertiser, 141
Boston Evening Transcript, 221
Bradford, Augustus, 182
Brady, Mathew, *177*; *4, 18, 22, 38, 50, 87, 94, 138, 147, 180, 190–193, 204, 212, 213, 219*
Brandy Station, 167
Bright, John, 51
Brooks, Noah, 58, *59*, 65, 88
Brough, John, 181
Bryant, William Cullen, 46, 205
Buchanan, James, 143
Buford, General John, 166, 168
Bull Run, battle of, 80, 82
burial of Gettysburg dead, *10, 11–13,* 32, *35–36,* 109, 162. *See also* Gettysburg National Cemetery
Burns, John, 168–169, 218, *219*
Burnside, General Ambrose Everett, 82, 115
Butler, Preston, *154*

Cameron, Simon, 65, 86, 182
Carpenter, Francis B., *50*

Causes and Conduct of the War, The (Everett), 188
Cemetery Ridge (Cemetery Hill), 156, 159, 169–170, 171, 173–175
Chancellorsville, battle of, 166, 167
Chase, Kate, 43, *44*
Chase, Salmon P., 43, 85, 86, 89
Chattanooga, battles at, 6–7
Chesapeake Bay, 79
Christian Commission of Philadelphia, 32
Civil War: 1863 course of, 6–7, 81, 166; early months of, 80, 81; and Emancipation Proclamation, 82; and battle of Gettysburg, 166–167 (*see also* Gettysburg, battle of)
Clay, Henry, 209
Cobb, Josephine, *190–193*
Coburn, Abner, 182
Cochrane, Lieutenant Henry, 76, 77, 79
Constitutional Union party, 185, 187
Cook, Elenora, 182
Cook, Sarah, 182
Cooper Union, AL's speech at, 98
Couch, General Darius, 109, 159
Culp's Hill, 159, 170, 173
Cunningham, W. H., 215
Curtin, Andrew, 12, 34, 36, *121*–122; 158–159; as Willses' guest, 39, 118, 122; and train to Gettysburg, 99, 100; at ceremony, 182, 189, *192–193*; son of, 158, 189, *192–193*
Cuthbert, Mary Ann, 29

Declaration of Independence. *See* "all men are created equal" clause
Dennison, William, 181
Devil's Den, 159, 172–173
Diamond, the (Gettysburg town square), 109, 158, 159
Douglas, Stephen A., *147*; AL's characterization of, 63; as public speaker, 71, 211; at AL's inauguration, 98; and Mary Todd, 98, 142; and Kansas-Nebraska Act, 142; debates AL, 145–146; beats AL for Senate, 146, 149; on slavery, *148*
Dred Scott decision, 143, 145

Eagle Hotel (Gettysburg), 46
Eckert, John, 96
Edwards, Ninian, 60
Emancipation Proclamation, 82, 92, 223. *See also* slavery, AL on
Emmitsburg road, 159, *160*, 175
Everett, Edward, *186*, *204*; chosen as Gettysburg keynote speaker, 34, 188–189; travels to Gettysburg, 39, 113, 115, 122; and AL, 58, *59*, 113, 187–188, 201; attends Gettysburg ceremony, 182–185, *184*, 189, *192–193*, 196, *197*, 198, *199*; life of, 185–189; delivers oration, 198–203; on Whitman, 205; and AL's Gettysburg Address, 214, 221, 224, 229–230
Everett copy (of Gettysburg Address), 229–230, *236–237*, 242–253
Ewell, General Richard, 169–170

Fifth New York Artillery Band, 113, 161
Fillmore, Millard, 185
Ford's Theater, 42–43
Forney, John, 110, 116, 181, 182
Fort Sumter, 80, 100
Frank Leslie's Illustrated Newspaper, 216
Fredericksburg, battle of, 81
Freese, Jacob R., 42
Frémont, John C., 143
French, Benjamin B., 45; and Gettysburg ceremonies, 46, 47, 182, 189, *192–193*, 195, *197*, 218; dirge composed by, 203, 205
Fry, General James B., 67, 94

Gardner, Alexander, 8, 72, 73, 83, *177*, *180*. *See also* Gardner brothers
Gardner brothers (Alexander and James), 30; gallery of, *56*; photographs by, 55–56, *57*, *58*, *59*, *64*. *See also* Gardner, Alexander
Gardner, James. *See* Gardner brothers
gatehouse (to Gettysburg town cemetery), *199*, *206*, 207–208
Getty, James, 108
Gettysburg, battle of, *106*, 162, 165–166, 168–176; significance, 6; the wounded,

7, 9, *11*, 171–172, 176; the dead, *8–10*, 11–12, *172*, 173; battlesites, *8, 9*, 159, 170–175; animals killed, 11, *163, 171*, 173; burial activities after, 12–13, 32, *35–36*; Lee's escape after, 26–28, 65, 176; events leading to, 166–168; Meade's headquarters during, *171*; and cemetery gatehouse, 207–208
Gettysburg, town of, *31*; after battle, 7, 9, *106*, 162; history of, 108; roads radiating from, 108, *155*, 168; on eve of ceremony, 109; 113–114, 118, 120–121; on morning of ceremony, 155–156; cemetery gatehouse in, *199, 206*, 207–208
Gettysburg Address: and Bible, 42, 135; language of, 60–61, 209; theme of, 111, 113; and AL's 1838 Springfield speech, 135–137; AL's pessimism about, 207, 220, 225, 230; delivery of, 208–209, 211, 214; AL's departure from text of, 209; variant versions of, 214–215, 227–253; immediate response to, 215–216, 220, 224–225; subsequent response to, 217–218, 221–222; simplicity of, 222; place in history of, 222–224; official version of, 231. *See also under* Lincoln, Abraham
Gettysburg College, *108*
Gettysburg Compiler, 166
Gettysburg National Cemetery, 13, 32–33, *35–36*; map of, *33. See also following entry*
Gettysburg National Cemetery, dedication of, *180, 184, 190–193*, 195–196, 198–203, *199*, 205, 207–216, *210, 216*; AL's view of, 5; planning of, 34; AL invited to, 36–37, 39, 41, 68; procession to, 157–159, *160*, 161–162, 164, 179, 181; speaker's platform at, 179, 181–182; guests at, 181–182; Everett at, 182–185, *184*, 189, *192–193, 199*, 200–203, 205; printed program for, 198; number attending, 198–199; flag at, *199*; closing of, 218. *See also preceding entry*
Giddings, J. R., 78
Gilbert, Joseph L., 215, 227, 228, 231

Gilbert report (of Gettysburg Address), 215, 227, 228, 231, 242–253
Globe Tavern (Springfield), 15
Governors' Special (train), 100, 118
Grant, Ulysses S., 6–7, 159, 166
Greeley, Horace, 52

Hale, Charles, 214, 227, 228, 231
Hale, Edward Everett, 214
Hale, Sarah Josepha, 35
Hale report (of Gettysburg Address), 214, 227, 228, 231, 242–253
Halleck, General Henry, 26–28, 64, 65
Hanks, Dennis, 126, *128*, 130
Hanks, Nancy, 126, 128, 130
Hanover, Pa., *35, 69*, 100–101
Hanover Junction, Pa., *69*, 99–100
Hardin County, Ky., 126
Harper, Robert G., 115, 120
Harpers Ferry, battle at, 80
Hay, John, 30, 49, 93, 149, 228; photographs of, *56, 57, 58, 112*; at Gettysburg, 110–111, 116, 161, *192–193*, 196
Hay draft (of Gettysburg Address), 228–229, *232–233*, 242–253
Hazel, Caleb, 129
Henry, Patrick, 61
Herndon, William C. (Billy), 53, *54*, 61, 201, 211, 213
Hesler, Alexander, *144*
Heth, General Henry, 166, 168
Holmes, Oliver Wendell, 61–62
Hooker, Joseph, 65, 82, 166, 167–168

Invalid Corps, 42, 68, 93
Iron Brigade, 168

Jackson, Andrew, 51, 89
Jackson, Calvin, *148*
Jackson, Lieutenant Fred, 93
Jackson, Stonewall, 81, 82, 166, 169
Jacobs, Michael, 183
Jefferson, Thomas, 26
Johnston, Sarah Bush, 130, *153*

Kansas-Nebraska Act, 142
Knox, William, 62

Lamon, Sally, 42

Lamon, Ward Hill, 30, 37, *38*, 109; appointed Gettysburg chief marshal, 37, 39, 42; as chief marshal, 45, 46–47, 158, 161, 181–182, 189, *192–193*, 198, 209; closeness to AL, 45, 46; violence of, 45–46; and Gettysburg Address, 65–66, 225; introduces AL, 205, 207

"Last Leaf" (Holmes), 62

Leaves of Grass (Whitman), 205

Lee, Robert E., 25, 26, 81, 82, 90, 166–170, 173–176

"Lexington" (Holmes), 61

Libby Prison, 110

Life of Washington (Weems), 131, 209

Lincoln, Abraham

    GETTYSBURG ADDRESS PREPARATION: first inspiration, 24; and July 7 talk, 25–26; invitation to speak, 36–37, 39; time available for, 39; brevity required, 39, 58; preoccupation with, 41–42, 43, 45, 47; and Everett text, 58, *59*, 201; tone decided on, 63; during final days before departure, 65–66; during train trip, 94, 97, 99; on eve of ceremony, 117–118, 121–122; Seward's counsel, 118, 120; and AL's life experience, 125; on morning of ceremony, 157; during Everett oration, 202–203. *See also* Gettysburg Address

    GETTYSBURG TRIP, 7; and Tad's illness, 3, 5, 24, 67, 68, 115, 122, 159; invitation extended, 36–37, 39, 41, 68; one-day journey rejected, 67; departure from Washington, 68–69; route of, *69*, 71; AL's state of health, 71, 93, 220; train accommodations, 71, 95; companions, 79–80, 85, 93–94, 107; through Baltimore, 95–96; through Hanover Junction, 99–100; at Hanover, 100–101; arrival in Gettysburg, 107, 109; return home, 220; smallpox attack, 220

    AT GETTYSBURG: Wills's invitation, 39; evening before ceremony, 109, 113–123; morning of ceremony, 156–157; in procession, 157–159, 161–162, 164, 181; on speaker's platform, 181–182, 184, *190–193*; during ceremonies, 196, 198; introduced by Lamon, 205; delivers address, 207–216; after ceremonies, 218, 220

    PERSONAL LIFE AND CHARACTERISTICS: death dreams, 17; reading habits, 19, 30, 42, 52, 61–63, 131, 142; summer retreat, *29–30*; horseback rides, 29–30; Bible and prayer, 24, 42, 52, 131; height, 48, *70*, 71, 72, *73*; humor, 49, 62–63, 68, 76, 95–96, 126; lack of organization, 52; intellect, 52–54, 60, 130–131, 142; disregard for formalities, 53; eating habits, 53, 58, 60; reluctance to aid biographers, 54–55; memory, 60; as poet, 61; as public speaker, 61, 71, 101, 114, 200–201, 208–209, 211; use of animal imagery, 63–65; strength, 71; hands and feet, *74*, *75*; face, 75–76, *82*, *83*, 154, 211–213, 226; aging, 76; as newspaper reader, 77; high hat, *96–97*, 98, 158; clothes, 97–98; preferred forms of address, 100–101; secretaries' names for, 111; episodes of melancholy, 133–134, 137, 141

    FAMILY AND MARRIAGE: son Tad's illness, 3, 5, 24, 67, 115, 122, 159; wife Mary, 3–5, 19, 28–29, 43, 58, 114, 140–141; feelings toward sons, 15–16, 17, 21, 23–24, 28–29; death of son Eddie, 16–17; death of son Willie, 17, 19–20, 67, 184–185; house owned by, *102*, *103*, *150*; dog Fido, *139*; and news of nomination, 149–150. *See also individual family members*

    EARLY LIFE AND CAREER: forebears, 125–126; childhood, 126, 129–132; on the Mississippi, 132; to Illinois, 132–133; death of Ann Rutledge, 133–134; to Springfield, 134–135; Springfield law books, *135*; marries,

137; as circuit lawyer, 88, 137–139; in Springfield, 101, 104, 139–141; elected to House of Representatives, 141; campaigning for Taylor and aftermath, 141–142; Peoria antislavery speech, 142–143; runs for Senate and nominated for vice-presidency, 143; Lincoln-Douglas debates, 145–146; loses Senate race to Douglas, 146, 149; nominated for presidency, 71, 86, 149–154

PRESIDENCY: Gettysburg plans, 13, 34; and Meade, 26–28, 65; conduct of war, 30–31, 51, 81–82; proclaims Thanksgiving Day, 34–35; routine details, 41–42; meeting the people, 47–48, 49, 51; office arrangements, 48–49, *50*, 51–52; at start of Civil War, 80; defends wife, 82, 84; Emancipation Proclamation, 82, 92, 223; cabinet, 85–92; Baltimore assassination plot, *95*; salary, 96; and Everett, 187–188

POLITICAL VIEWPOINTS AND SPEECHES: on democracy, 79, 80, 113, 134; First Inaugural, 98, 119–120; and slavery, 132, 142–143, 145–146; first writings, 133; 1838 Springfield speech, 134–137; opposes Mexican War, 141; Peoria antislavery speech, 142–143; "house divided" speech, 145, 146, 223; Second Inaugural, 223–224. *See also* Gettysburg Address

ATTITUDES TOWARD: viewed as coarse and unserious, 37, 49, 68, 71, 152; congressional attacks, 82; Usher's, 89; Everett's, 113, 187; Seward's, 120; history's, 223–224

PHOTOGRAPHS OF, *50, 55–56, 57, 58, 59, 64, 70, 72, 73, 83, 140, 144, 148, 154, 190–193, 212–213, 226*

Lincoln, Abraham (grandfather of AL), 126

Lincoln, Edward (Eddie; son), 15–17, 21

Lincoln, John (great-grandfather), 126

Lincoln, Mary Todd (wife), *4, 136*; and son Tad's illness, 3, 5, 67; tantrums of, 5; and children, 16; and son Willie, 17, 19–21, 67; and son Eddie, 17, 21; insanity of, 19, 140–141; and spiritualism, 21; summer trip by, 28; and Kate Chase, 43, *44*; and Benjamin French, 45; as housekeeper, 58, 151; accusations against, 82; and AL's appearance, 98; and Stephen Douglas, 98, 142; on AL's public speaking, 114; marriage of, 137; and belief in AL's destiny, 141–142; and AL's presidential nomination, 149–150

Lincoln, Mordecai, elder and younger (ancestors), 126

Lincoln, Nancy Hanks (mother), 126, 128, 130

Lincoln, Robert Todd (son), *14*, 15–16, 17, 28, 221

Lincoln, Samuel (ancestor), 125–126

Lincoln, Sarah (sister), 129, 130, 132

Lincoln, Sarah Bush Johnston (Sally; stepmother), 130, *153*

Lincoln, Thomas (father), 126, *127*, 129–130, 132, 153

Lincoln, Thomas (Tad; son), 17, 21, 22, *23*–24, 28, *102*; illness of, 3, 5, 24, 67, 115, 122, 159; and AL's presidential nomination, 149, 150, 151–152

Lincoln, William Wallace (Willie; son), *18*, 19–21, 81, *102*, 149, 150, 151–152, 184–185

Lincoln-Douglas debates, 63, 145–146

Little Round Top, *8*, 99, 159, 172, 173, 175

Logan, Stephen T., 42

Longfellow, Henry Wadsworth, 46, 205

Longstreet, General James, 82, 174–175

Lookout Mountain, attack on, 6, 7

McClellan, General George B., 37, 72, 82

McClernand, General John A., *73*

McDougall, William, 157

McDowell, General Irvin, 82

McIlheny, R. F., 166

MacVeagh, Wayne, 107, 110, 116, 196, 220

Marble Heart, The (play), 43

Meade, General George Gordon, 27; and battle of Gettysburg, 9, 30, 168, 169, 170, 173–174; and Lee's escape, 26–28, 65, 176; and Gettysburg ceremonies, 161, 196, 198
medical care at Gettysburg, 11, 171–172
Mercier, Henri, 93, 94
Mexican-American War, 81–82, 141
Missionary Ridge, attack at, 6
Miss Leslie's Lady's House-Book, 96
Missouri Compromise, 142
Missouri Republican, 227
Morris, General William, 95
Morton, Oliver Perry, 182

Napoleon, Prince, 20
Nasby, Petroleum V., 63
New England, AL's speaking tour in, 141
New Salem, Ill., 132
newspapers, 42, 76–77, 181, 221–222. See also individual newspapers
New York World, 37
Nicolay, John, 93, 101, 157, 213, 228; photographs of, 56, 57, 58, 111; at Gettysburg, 110, 157, 161, 189, 192–193
Nicolay draft (of Gettysburg Address), 228–229, 234–235, 242–253

Oregon Territory, 142
O'Sullivan, Timothy, 8, 177, 219

Parker, Joel, 182
Parker, Theodore, 61
Peach Orchard, 159, 172–173
Peel, Sir Robert, 198
Pennsylvania College of Gettysburg (Gettysburg College), 108
Philadelphia Inquirer, 101, 227
Photographic Incidents of the War (Gardner brothers), 55–56
Pickett, General George, 173–176
Pierce, Franklin, 142
Pinkerton, Allan, 73, 95
Polk, James, 141
Poore, Benjamin Perley, 182
Pope, General John, 64
Provost, Colonel Charles M., 161

Rebert, James A., 157
Riney, Zachariah, 129
Rutledge, Ann, 132, 133–134

Saunders, William, 32, 33, 182
Schenck, General James Findlay, 95, 161
Scott, Dred, 143
Scott, General Winfield, 81–82, 161
Scovill, Joseph, 37
Seminary Ridge, 159, 170, 173–174
Senate, U.S., 82, 84
Seward, William Henry, 85, 86, 90, 91, 92, 157, 187; and Willie Lincoln, 20; and AL's Thanksgiving proclamation, 35; on AL's office hours, 48; and AL, 89, 92, 120; and Baltimore, 95; at Gettysburg, 110, 115, 161, 182, 192–193, 207; and Gettysburg Address, 118, 120, 224; and AL's First Inaugural Address, 119
Seymour, Horatio, 159, 182
Shead, Carrie, 108
Shepherd, N. H., 136, 140
Sherman, William Tecumseh, 7, 159
Showacre, John W., 69
Sickles, General Daniel, 172
Sisters of Charity, 32
Slade, William, 117–118
Slaughter-Pen, 9
slavery, AL on, 132, 142–143, 145–146. See also Emancipation Proclamation
smallpox, 220
Smith, Caleb Blood, 85, 86, 87
Soldiers' National Cemetery. See Gettysburg National Cemetery
Speed, James, 65
Speed, Joshua, 15–16, 137, 138
Sprague, William, 43
Springfield, Ill.: AL's departure from, 101, 104; train station of, 105; AL's life in, 134–135, 139–141; and AL's nomination, 149–151, 150
Stahel, General Julius, 159
Staley, Andrew B., 95
Stanton, Edwin, 30, 67, 115; son of, 93, 110
State Journal (Springfield, Ill.), 227

Stockton, T. H., 93, 182, *192–193*, 195–196
Stuart, General Jeb, 82, 167, 168
Sumner, Charles, 63

Taylor, Zachary, 141
Thanksgiving Day, AL's proclamation of, 34–35
Thomas, General George Henry, 7
Thucydides, 200
Tod, David, 181, 182
Todd, Mary. *See* Lincoln, Mary Todd
Townsend, George Alfred, 48
Tyson brothers, *180*

Ulke, Henry, 89
United States, events of 1863 in, 7, 78–79
United States Senate, 82, 84
Usher, John Palmer, 85, *87*–89, 161, 182, 189, *192–193*

Vicksburg, battle of, 25, 166

Washington, D.C., 28–29, 51, 76–77
Washington, George, 60, 104, 185, 202
"We Are Coming, Father Abraham" (hymn), 118, 123

Weaver brothers (Frank and Samuel), *35, 180*
Webster, Daniel, 61
Weems, Mason Locke, 131, 209
Welles, Gideon, 85, 86
Wheat-Field, *8*, 159, 172–173
Whipple, John Adams, *102*
White House, *23*
Whiting's War Powers, 52
Whitman, Walt, 5, 205
Whittier, John Greenleaf, 46, 205
Willis, Nathaniel P., 19–*20*
Wills, David, *12*–13, 32; as ceremonies planner, 34, 37, 39, 46, 118, 157, 161; as host, 39, *55*, 109, 113–114, 115, 118, 121, 218; at ceremonies, 182, 189, *192–193*; and Everett, 183
Wills, Mrs. David, *114*
Wise, Charlotte (Charlie), 93, 122, 182, 183–184
Worcester, Mass., 141
world events of 1863, 5–6, 7, 77–79

Yates, Richard, 78
Young, John Russell, 182, 224
Young Men's Lyceum of Springfield, 134